Predestination

Predestination

A Guide for the Perplexed

Jesse Couenhoven

t&t clark

LONDON · NEW YORK · OXFORD · NEW DELHI · SYDNEY

T&T CLARK
Bloomsbury Publishing Plc
50 Bedford Square, London, WC1B 3DP, UK
1385 Broadway, New York, NY 10018, USA

BLOOMSBURY, T&T CLARK and the T&T Clark logo are trademarks of
Bloomsbury Publishing Plc

First published in Great Britain 2018

A catalogue record for this book is available from the British Library.

A catalog record for this book is available from the Library of Congress.

ISBN: HB: 978-0-5676-2995-1
PB: 978-0-5670-5471-5
ePDF: 978-0-5672-4966-1
ePub: 978-0-5673-2403-0

Typeset by Newgen KnowledgeWorks Pvt. Ltd., Chennai, India
Printed and bound in Great Britain

To find out more about our authors and books visit www.bloomsbury.com and
sign up for our newsletters.

For Amy. It wasn't love at first sight, but you can't escape destiny forever.

CONTENTS

ACKNOWLEDGMENTS

Quite a few people have waited patiently for me to finish this book for some time now. Some of them have even refrained from making jokes about whether I was really predestined to write it. First among those is my wife, Amy Tsou, without whose help and advice I might write more quickly but also more poorly. My son Ian does not understand about writing books but he will nevertheless be pleasantly surprised that I am wrestling with its contents less and him more. I am grateful to my parents, David and Sarah Couenhoven, as well, for the interest they have shown in this project. Many colleagues and friends (which are not meant to be mutually exclusive categories) have given me advice and encouragement along the way, and even read portions of the manuscript. My thanks to Peter Busch, John Bowlin, John Churchill, Adam Eitel, Mary Hirschfield, Kevin Hughes, Matthew Levering, Charles Mathewes, Joshua Mauldin, Gerald McKenny, Gilbert Meilaender, Justin Nickel, Douglas Ottati, Matthew Puffer, Edmund Santurri, Thomas Smith, Kirsi Stjerna, Aku Visala, Olli-pekka Vainio, William Werpehowski, James Wetzel, and Brett Wilmot. I particularly want to thank the Templeton Foundation, Florida State University, and Alfred Mele for supporting the early stages of my work on this project through a "Big Questions in Free Will" grant. Finally, I am grateful to Bloomsbury Press and my editor, Anna Turton, who have been the most patient of all.

For permission to use portions of articles I have previously published I want to thank the presses and editors who originally published them. The introduction makes use of "Predestination." In *Vocabulary for the Study of Religion*, edited by Robert Segal and Kocku von Stuckrad, Boston: Brill Publishers, 2015, pp. 115–117. Ch. 4 contains elements of "The Augustinian Background of Luther's *Bondage of the Will*." In *On the Apocalyptic and Human*

Agency: Conversations with Augustine of Hippo and Martin Luther, edited by Kirsi Stjerna and Deanna Thompson, Newcastle upon Tyne: Cambridge Scholars Press, 2014, pp. 93–102; and "The Protestant Reformation." In the *Cambridge History of Moral Philosophy*, edited by Sacha Golob and Jens Timmermann, Cambridge: Cambridge University Press, 2017, pp. 208–220.

Introduction

It lies not in our power to love or hate,
For will in us is overruled by fate.
When two are stripped, long ere the course begin,
We wish that one should love, the other win;
And one especially do we affect
Of two gold ingots, like in each respect:
The reason no man knows; let it suffice
What we behold is censured by our eyes.
Where both deliberate, the love is slight:
Who ever loved, that loved not at first sight?
CHRISTOPHER MARLOWE, HERO AND LEANDER

1. The promise of predestination

To modern sensibilities, the doctrine of predestination seems both strange and problematic. Given our scientific progress, our control of nature, and the degree of self-determination available to the citizens of the democracies leading the world, it seems odd to claim that matters of ultimate importance may yet be in God's hands. Moreover, it seems unfair to claim that God might bless or curse our lives even if we could not have chosen to make them turn out differently. It would be easy to dismiss this doctrine (like seemingly related talk about fate or astrology) as a relic of an unenlightened past, a day when humanity really was more helpless than it is today. Perhaps our ancestors felt their lack and mistakenly ascribed it to a distinction between the finite and the infinite.

The motivating hypothesis of this book, however, is that it is an act of hubris to dismiss the idea of predestination without studying it more carefully than, in recent times, we have. Because the doctrine of predestination is now typically characterized as the pessimistic conviction of Calvinists who denigrate human agency, it may come as a surprise to be reminded that predestination has actually been defended by most of the great Catholic and Protestant minds of the past, and by many leading Muslim and Jewish intellectuals as well.[1] Surely they cannot all simply be dismissed as mere pessimists or fools. We ought, at least, to attempt to see what might have attracted great minds throughout history to espouse this doctrine. Then we will be in a better position to consider whether our world is as different from theirs as it can appear to be. Once we give this doctrine more than a cursory glance, it may begin to strike us—at least, it has begun to strike me—that it contains a good deal of insight into aspects of the human condition that vary only a little with time.

Given the ways in which doctrines of predestination have been used and abused throughout its history, it is not hard to understand why one might have reservations about them. Even people of faith have learned to be wary of those who say they see hints of a divine hand in the events that come to pass around us. When "prophets" arise who seek to proclaim that the events of history are part of some greater story being told by God, they typically make their coreligionists squirm (and nonbelievers jeer). The fact that their attempts to explain why history has taken its peculiar course often seem arbitrary and ad hoc has not strengthened their cause.[2] The great religious leaders of the past did not, however, equate their belief in predestination with the claim that they understood or could explain the currents of history to any great degree. Still less did they mean to claim that they knew the spiritual meaning of individual events. Rather, they saw in the doctrine of predestination an affirmation of a more general relationship between God and ultimate human ends, a relationship of love that precedes merit.

One way to reintroduce ourselves to the ancient idea of predestination is to remember the way we still talk about "falling" in love. As C. S. Lewis noted in a famous treatise on *The Four*

Loves, "half the love songs and half the love poems in the world will tell you that the Beloved is your fate or destiny, no more your choice than a thunderbolt, for 'it is not in our power to love or to hate'."[3] This is particularly intriguing because although lovers fall, helplessly, they do not mind. In romantic love it seems appropriate, somehow, for significant events to occur that are out of our control. Indeed, it is widely felt that it is more delightful for things to be that way. The best loves are those that feel preordained, as if fitted to us from eternity. Such loves are more stumbled upon than planned or chosen. They overtake us. Perhaps if a kind of predestining can be good in such a central area of life—our deepest relationships—we should take seriously the possibility that it could be a good in others, too.

Even today, *eros* is widely spoke of as involving some kind of destiny, and of course we know that for the most part our families are bestowed on us as a gift not a choice. Still, we do typically think that we are in control of choosing our friends. But that too, Lewis argued, is an illusion:

> A few years' difference in the dates of our births, a few more miles between houses, the choice of one university rather than another, posting to different regiments, the accident of one topic being raised or not raised at a first meeting—any of these chances might have kept us apart.[4]

Our friendships might not seem to fall like a thunderbolt from the sky, the way romantic love or desire can. Friendships are nevertheless more given to us than they are the deserved and fitting product of our own meritorious effort. Like romantic love, friendship is "not a reward for our discrimination and good taste" but "the instrument by which God reveals to each the beauties of all the others."[5] Lewis insisted that those who believe in God have a particular obligation to be aware of our lack of control over all our most significant relationships: "for a Christian, there are, strictly speaking, no chances. A secret Master of ceremonies has been at work."[6]

In Lewis's appropriation of ancient Christian claims about the gift-character of both our friendships and our romances, we catch a glimpse of the fundamental religious stance of gratitude that the doctrine of predestination is meant to express. The events in our lives that evoke love and appreciation are not fundamentally accidental, but nor are they self-made. They are, instead, a feast, at which God has spread the table. The idea that this feast is not something that we can or should work up for ourselves, but are rather called to embrace and enjoy, suggests that there are goods it is better to be given than to take for oneself. It may be somewhat easier for us to understand predestination's appeal when we see it from this vantage point. The doctrine does not necessarily express the deterministic conviction that everything happens as God intends. It does, however, affirm that the most important things in life are under God's care in very specific ways. In the midst of many penultimate sorrows, belief in predestination offers the hope that our lives are ultimately in hands more capable than our own.

2. Some questions about predestination

Prominent defenders of doctrines of predestination have thought of it as a story about a God who makes and renews creation out of love. It might, however, seem facile to make too much of analogies between predestination and happy topics like love. The doctrine has been thought by many modern commentators (and some ancient ones) to cast a dark shadow over the theologians who defend it. The main reason for this is that the idea of predestination raises deep questions about creaturely freedom and divine responsibility for evil. As we will see, these questions have been asked since Augustine first articulated his influential doctrine of predestination. We will see, too, that historic theologians who defended doctrines of predestination were not simply confounded by these questions, but offered thoughtful (if often incomplete) responses to them.

This book mainly focuses on the problems and promise of human predestination. Here I introduce some key questions about predestination by reflecting on another historically central battleground: the theological puzzle of how and why the devil fell from the state of grace in which he was created. Intriguingly, the Fall of the angels provided a framework for discussion of the predestination of the saints in the work of Augustine, Aquinas, and other ancient theologians who speculated that among the reasons for the predestination of human beings was that they would fill up the gap in heaven's company left by the demons.[7] This was by no means the only reason for predestination in the human case, nor was it the most important. Still, they counted it a factor among God's motivations in predestining the church.

A natural place to begin any discussion of the devil's fall is with the famous depiction of Satan in Dante's *Inferno*.[8] Dante imagined Satan as at once the responsible agent of his revolt against God and helplessly doomed to fail in that revolt. The Lucifer of his poem is a winged beast incarcerated not in a place of fire but in a hell made of ice. Ironically, Lucifer's prison is of his own making, the result of his foolishly proud attempt to separate himself from God. The frantic beating of his massive wings as he endlessly tries to flee the divine presence creates a cold wind that freezes the water in the air around him. Because he is the architect of his own punishment, were he to stop fleeing and return to God, the block of ice that entraps him would melt, and he would no longer be in hell.

In Dante's story, Satan's fault is clear. Yet so also is a kind of destiny. Because Satan was created by God to be a certain kind of being, Satan cannot make himself into whatever he pleases. Dante does not argue that Lucifer's choice to rebel against God was predestined, but he does suggest that it cannot succeed. Dante's story of Creation and Fall thus incorporates a destiny. The fact that certain aspects of the future seem to be set is among the factors that gives Satan's story a powerfully tragic aspect. The reader can see that Satan's attempt to be a power autonomous from God is doomed to fail even if the perpetually falling angel lacks such insight.

Being doomed to fail if he makes an evil choice is a very limited sort of destiny, however, different from simply being doomed to fail. Typically, doctrines of predestination claim not merely that the outcomes of one's choices are not under one's control, but that one's most significant actions themselves might be preordained in some way or other. Such claims imply that even if not everything is determined, some of the events in our individual and communal histories had to happen. That would presumably include not only positive events such as salvation or resurrection but also negative events such as suffering, death, and even the fall into sin itself (especially if those positive events require the negative events in order to be possible). Yet if the Fall is in some way part of God's plan, as doctrines of predestination usually imply, that can appear to undermine the claim that the Fall is blameworthy. If God plans for the Fall even prior to creating, does that not make Satan's proud choices lose their primacy in the order of explanation? God becomes implicated in evil as much as Satan, or more.

Interestingly, however, it is not only predestinarian tellings of the Fall that raise difficult questions. Because Satan always acts in a manner responsive to a setting already put in place by God, every rendition of the Fall story raises questions about divine responsibility and goodness. It is, after all, quite odd that the angels, who are supposed to be rational beings of great power and insight, would have revolted against God's authority because, thinking too highly of themselves, they desired to be masters of their own fates. It seems that they should have known better than to believe that such autonomy constituted true freedom.[9] How could they fall into the trap of believing that they knew better than their maker—and why would God let them? A primal sin of pride, seeking autonomy, raises as many questions as it answers, and even the claim that the devil fell by a free choice leaves us perplexed.

Inspired by the awed and grateful question in Psalm 8 "What is man that you are mindful of him?," some Jewish and Christian theologians have tried to shed light on what made the Fall psychologically possible by adding some additional details to the story. They have speculated that the angels who abandoned trust in God's leadership did so not merely out of pride but because they were jealous and even repulsed when they found out about God's plan for creation.[10] God, they discovered, intended to elevate finite, fleshly human beings above the angels, and to give them powers (such as reproduction) that the angels lacked. It is not hard to imagine that such a plan would have seemed unwise, unfair, and inelegant to the angels. According to this version of the Fall story, the difference between the angels who fell and those who did not comes down to a distinction between those who patiently placed themselves in God's hands and waited for the story of creation to unfold, and those who sought to make things "better" by writing their own counternarratives. Satan took the revolt a step further with his successful attempt to seduce the humans whom God had created into a prideful disobedience of their own. In order to separate them from God, he told them to think for themselves, rather than trust God's command. Satan engaged in this trickery not simply to create trouble for God, but to get back at humans. It is ironically quite apt that he maneuvered God into cursing the very human power of reproduction he had envied in the first place. Here, it seems, he had scored quite a victory.

This elaboration on the Fall story is a compelling, if speculative, attempt to give Lucifer a motive for his otherwise baffling rebellion against his own creator. The most obvious point it makes is that evil never happens in a vacuum. The desire to live a life apart from a God whose decrees seem unjust or aesthetically displeasing might be foolish but it is not unintelligible. If God's plan for creation put the angels (and later humans) in a position that required them to trust without fully understanding what God was up to, it is easier for us to see why they might have fallen. The Fall becomes psychologically plausible.

But although this traditional development of the Fall story offers some clarity on the question of why otherwise wise and good angels might have chosen to defy God, it does not simply encourage a "free choice" reading of the Fall. Indeed, it not only continues to raise questions about how much control the angels had over their fall into sin, but also highlights the possibility that sin is provoked and even perhaps in some way guided by God. As God must have known it would, his proposal to honor human beings with undeserved status offended the angels who sought to organize the universe according to a simple measure of justice, one that left no place for grace. The angels' attitude certainly makes them look less than entirely admirable, but it also directs our attention once again toward divine nature. Given that God is supposed to be full of mercy and compassion, it seems highly ironic that it was grace itself that provoked the Fall. Why did God not constitute the angels such that they too were gracious, or at least better able to understand the role of grace in the order of things? Why did God not explain the divine plan more fully? The angels who became devils may have lacked charity, but their lack seems to point behind them, to their creator, who might have led them more gently. Thus, it remains natural to wonder to what degree the angels' fall should be considered their fault. If God knew that the divine grace bestowed on the undeserving would provoke the angels to envy, in what way did the angels who fell have significant agency? Once again, if God made sin part of some complex overall plan, it is not hard to see the plausibility of an argument that the ultimate explanation for the Fall, and responsibility for it, actually rests in God's hands.

This concern is reinforced if we recall what happens next in the traditional Fall story: after the Fall, God curses the woman's powers of reproduction and the man's labor, but then utters a greater curse against the devil, one that foretells that out of this apparent victory Satan's defeat will be born. Satan's attempt to revolt against God may initially appear to be a success, but ironically it is revealed to contain the seeds of its own failure, and in two ways. First, as we have seen, God has so constituted creation that pride is necessarily self-undermining; it is the sin of those who are too psychologically weak to wait upon the Lord. What looks like empowered if rebellious angelic agency, then, is really a lack of genuine power. Second, Satan's pride provides the setting in which God begins to fulfill the plan announced from the beginning, to elevate human beings. As later developments in the story clarify, God counters the human Fall and redeems procreation by associating humanity with divinity in the person of Jesus Christ. Thus, it appears that even the angels who seek to thwart God are caught up in serving God's plan. Much like Judas in his later attempt to betray Jesus, Satan is God's servant precisely in his attempt to be autonomous, and what presumably appeared to him like an independent choice turns out to be anything but. Satan's fall sets a pattern that Christians see repeated again and again, as revolts against God turn out to serve the divine plan in surprising yet poetically apt ways.

Perhaps largely because scripture appears to indicate both that the fallen angels really are to blame and that nothing happens outside of God's overarching plan, theologians have neither typically wanted to say that the Fall can simply be explained by reference to the angels' independent choices, nor have they solely made reference to God's intentions. They agree, then, that both God and the angels factor into any genuine explanation for the Fall (analogous points can be made about the human fall). However, they have gone about holding these claims together in contrasting ways.

On the view that has become most popular in our day, theologians have suggested that God makes the angels ignorant of the full divine intent, and able to fall into pride, in order to offer the angels a self-determining choice. Keeping them "in the dark" was, on this account, actually an act of grace that made it possible for the angels to have their own independent agency. If they trust, or do not trust, that decision was up to them, not determined by God.

Thus, although they were created by a power outside themselves, their ultimate moral and spiritual status was in their own hands. On this "free choice" view the angels are ultimately the authors of their own stories, because they have a genuine sovereignty over the sphere of their activity. Placing such power in the hands of creatures might seem to undermine the ability of those who put their trust in God to confidently believe that goodness will absolutely prevail, but it may be enough that God's power and creativity makes it possible for evil to be defeated in more limited ways.[11] Today, many believers are willing to trade the ancient hope that the history of the world is ordered in some poetic and apt manner for the possibility that although what we have become may be a collective accident of some sort, it is one that has individually been self-made.

By contrast, the view that has historically been most popular in the Christian tradition influenced by St. Augustine suggests that God is able to work out ways to make even betrayal serve greater goods because God is as much the author of the angels' stories as they are. In some sense, they are coauthors, and the angels' activity is subject to the overlapping magisterium of God's activity. On this view, God's responsibility for world history is real, but not in competition with the angels' own responsibility for their actions. This is because God's great and unique power and creativity allows the angels to have a genuine if secondary agency. Thus, God creates them with the power to be genuine actors in the world, but God does not give up ultimate direction and control over their stories (stories, it may be noted, about which we know only a little, which makes them difficult to understand or judge).

This second ("noncompetitive") view has traditionally accused the first (the "free choice" view) of echoing the very hubris that led to the angelic fall in the first place. At the same time, proponents of the free-choice view often accuse the noncompetitive approach of undermining created agency to the point that it encourages fatalism.[12] Proponents of the free-choice view typically defend their stance with the claim that their position does a better job of defending God against the charge of being the author of sin, and of respecting the mysterious roots of evil. The clearest way to demarcate the separation between Christian doctrine and fatalism may be to highlight undetermined human free choices. However, proponents of the noncompetitive view have typically replied that this separation can be demarcated in another way. Fate occurs without regard for human agency, but predestination cooperates with creaturely agency. The noncompetitive approach may also do a better job of recognizing the limits of our agency, while protecting the hope that evil will not prevail. It still faces an obvious problem of evil, however, particularly the question of why God would blame and punish evildoers who, if they are predestined, appear in some ways to be doing the divine will. As we will see, those theologians who subscribed to doctrines of predestination were not primarily interested in offering a theodicy. One reason for this was that they considered questions about God's relationship to evil to be a problem faced equally by all traditional theists, irrespective of whether they subscribe to a doctrine of predestination or not. These theologians were not, however, entirely lacking in resources for responding to the questions about evil raised by their views.

As this discussion of the devil's fall suggests, the points one can make for and against predestination are complex, and depend in part on what doctrine of predestination one has in mind. In my view, however, the greatest scandal of the doctrine of predestination in our day is not the inherently controversial nature of this most controversial of doctrines (which has always been a source of confusion, hope, and dissent) but that today so little informed discussion is to be heard contending for or against a view that many of the great theologians of the past considered essential to their faith.

A scientist in a novel by Arthur C. Clarke once asserted that religious claims can be destroyed by being ignored as well as by being disproven.[13] Plainly, the doctrine of predestination is as much under the former threat as the latter. In not taking the idea of predestination seriously, however, we have failed to wrestle with the deep ideas and questions associated with it.

In order to bring those issues to our attention once again, this book develops the logic of the idea of predestination, particularly as it has been articulated by figures central to the Augustinian tradition, who are the most well-known proponents of the doctrine. On my reading, Augustinian doctrines of predestination centrally rest on the (implicit) premise that *a human being's greatest good lies (not in having independent control of one's personal story but) in being a genuine actor in a narrative ultimately blessed by good relationships*. The Augustinian claims that such a good life need not lack freedom or responsibility, if those goods are properly understood. In fact, what draws Augustinian theologians to endorse their doctrines of predestination is not mainly a need to protect divine sovereignty but a conception of human agency, and its place in the created order, that raises profound questions about the extent and sort of authorial control we should aspire to have over ourselves. To appropriate Lewis's metaphor of the feast, the Augustinian suggestion is that a better life may be found in enjoying the complex flavours presented to us by a master chef than in subsisting on the inelegant mash we would make if left to our own devices.

The purpose of this book is to develop these ideas. My hope is to consider, not uncritically, what might be interesting, insightful, and worthwhile about leading doctrines of predestination, and also to examine whether some ways of developing those doctrines might be more attractive than others. In order to pursue that task as thoughtfully and succinctly as possible, the remainder of this introduction offers a few orienting remarks that aim to clarify how doctrines of predestination have differed, and to summarize what to expect from the chapters that follow this one.

3. Many predestinations

As the discussion above has begun to make clear, predestination is not simply the belief that God has a plan for your life, but the belief that God has always had such a plan, and will certainly effect that plan. Moreover, the plan in question is quite specific and significant: it is a plan for salvation, not merely a plan for other lesser goods. St. Augustine calls predestination a choice God made before the creation of the world, to bestow the benefits that liberate a person from sin and death.[14] This means that predestination includes but goes beyond divine foreknowledge. God not only knows in advance what is predestined but also elects in advance to act in a certain way and knows that certain things will come to pass because of that decision. Thus, God causes what will happen, not only by creating a particular world, out of all the possibilities God had in mind, but also by actively shaping that world's ongoing history and destiny.

This also means that a doctrine of predestination differs in important ways from a doctrine of divine providence. Belief in God's providence is the trust that God actively promotes the good of at least some of those in the creation. This is something God can do even if God does not predestine anyone to salvation. At the same time, predestination implies some sort of belief in the providence of God as well, since without divine providence God would not have a way to ensure that the plan of salvation is implemented. For many theologians, predestination is a special instance of a more general divine providence.

However, predestination does not necessarily imply complete divine determinism (though some theologians have believed in both). Determinism is the idea that current facts permit only one possible future; divine determinism is the idea that God has intentionally made it the case that there is only one possible future. If complete (or what philosophers sometimes call "global") divine determinism were true, everything that happens has to happen, and everything happens just as God ordained it to happen. The strongest form that a belief in divine providence and predestination could take would be a belief in divine determinism, but it is entirely possible to believe in weaker versions of a doctrine of providence or predestination. That said, predestination does imply that some facts about one's future are set—indeed, it implies that one's eternal destiny is set from the moment of creation. Thus, although predestination does not imply global divine determinism, it does mean that at least some things are determined by God.

Now that a little has been said to clarify how a doctrine of predestination relates to doctrines with which it is sometimes confused, it is important to outline some of the most important forms that doctrines of predestination have taken. Much ink has been spilt in arguments over the precise form a doctrine of predestination ought to take; the most important of those arguments concern how God determines the story of redemption, and what aspects of that story God determines.

Single predestination is the belief that God determines only those who will be saved. As I explain in the following chapter, with some caveats, this position appears to have been Augustine's. On this view, God does not predestine anyone to be damned. Satan's fall, like the human fall into sin, is either not destined or not ultimately determinative of sinners' final destinies. At the same time, the unsaved cannot save themselves, which raises some questions about the distinction between single and double predestination. One way to clarify the difference is to advocate an extreme (and uncommon) version of single predestination, according to which those who are not predestined to salvation have a kind of free will that allows them to turn to God for salvation. A third, more popular (though still historically rare) version of single predestination, one perhaps first suggested by Friedrich Schleiermacher, is the hope that God predestines everyone to be saved.[15]

Double predestination, conversely, is the belief that God decrees both who will be saved and who will be damned. John Calvin is the most famous proponent of this position. On the most extreme version of this view, God determines both salvation and damnation in the same way, as a positive action. A more common view, however, is that although God saves actively by working to ensure that those God has elected for salvation do not fall away, God damns passively, by leaving some sinners to their sin. Again, this means that the line between double and single predestination can be fuzzy, and it can be difficult to distinguish between these two views.

Further distinctions between predestinarian views offer contrasting speculation about God's logic in predestining. This may be the best place to mention that debates about predestination have at times become highly abstruse as well as polemical and pedantic.[16] In the course of such debates, some have even claimed that the doctrine of predestination is the linchpin of Christian systematic theology. Such arguments have not cast the doctrine into a favorable light, and may have had a good deal to do with its having fallen into disfavor. The doctrines of predestination considered in this book, by contrast, are less speculative and overreaching, and were for the most part developed much earlier in history than the sometimes highly polemical Puritan or Reformed scholastic approaches to predestination. Nevertheless, a distinction between ways of thinking about predestination that began to be offered long after most of the authors we will consider may be of some help as we try to sort out the implications of their views. That is the distinction between infra- and supra-lapsarianism. On the most common approach, that of infralapsarianism, the divine election of those who will be saved is conceptually dependent on prior divine decisions to create humanity and to permit the fall into sin, and thus responds to the human activity that God foresees. On supralapsarianism, divine election conceptually precedes the divine decision to create and permit sin, as well as human qualities. This view is meant to highlight the undeserved nature of both salvation and damnation.

Interestingly, both views seem to accept the premise (which Leibniz considered dubious) that God made each of these decisions in isolation, rather than electing them all together as part of a "series" of mutually implicating decrees.

4. Chapter overview

Not all of the doctrines of predestination just surveyed are discussed in the following chapters. Rather than offer a comprehensive survey of possible views, this book takes a sustained look at a handful of the most influential perspectives on predestination in the history of Christian thought. Perhaps not surprisingly, all of the authors considered are Augustinian in some deep way, although the points of their agreement and disagreement with Augustine have often been misunderstood. One aspiration of this book is to correct common misreadings of these authors. A correlated aim is to show that Augustine, Aquinas, Luther, and Calvin are not as far apart in their doctrines of predestination or their views about human agency as is widely thought. At the same time, the authors discussed do have significant differences, some of which I critique along the way or in the final, constructive chapter.

Chapter 1 begins with Augustine, the natural starting point for any discussion of predestination. Augustine was the first figure to fully articulate a doctrine about what he called the predestination of the saints, which he offered in part as an alternative to pagan conceptions of an indifferent universe. He developed his thinking not primarily for philosophical reasons but over a long period of wrestling with passages in the Bible that indicate God's sovereignty over world history and the priority of divine grace, which is given to biblical figures like Jacob even before it could be deserved. The core theological conviction behind Augustine's doctrine of predestination was that we cannot save ourselves but need the help of Christ. This was the implication not only of biblical teaching, Augustine concluded, but also of the practice of infant baptism, which offers a clear sacramental indication that everything depends on the divine initiative. Augustine did not, however, believe that human agency is simply eclipsed by the divine decree concerning who will become part of Christ's body. Rather, he argued that God elects to involve human beings in the course of history in crucial ways. In his attempts to explain how this is possible, Augustine developed the first richly detailed noncompetitive conception of the relationship between human and divine agency in Christian theology. On this view human persons are genuine agents, worthy of credit and blame, as long as they act out of their own reasons and loves. The fact that God can and does shape human hearts and minds need not detract from the significance of voluntary creaturely agency.

The following chapter discusses Anselm, who is often said to have been a follower of Augustine. On the topics that we consider, however, he broke with Augustine in several important ways. He offers a helpful point of contrast with Augustine, and a reminder that opposition to Augustine's doctrine of predestination is by no means a modern idiosyncrasy. For Anselm, unlike Augustine, human freedom and responsibility require the availability of undetermined, self-determining choices. As a result, Anselm did not want to follow Augustine's doctrine of grace more than halfway. He agreed that sinners cannot be saved without God's help, but he rejected the possibility of divine determination. Given Anselm's libertarian approach to human agency, it would have been easy for him to reject the idea of predestination altogether. However, Anselm attempted to reinterpret the idea of predestination in the light of divine foreknowledge. If God knows in advance what we freely choose, God is able to predestine without foreclosing our options, or forcing anyone to choose heaven or hell.

Anselm's view is attractive in many respects, but it stretches the meaning of the term "predestination" in ways that might seem odd to predestination's advocates and detractors alike. Thomas Aquinas, I argue in the third chapter, returned to a more recognizable view. In fact, Aquinas's view of predestination was almost exactly like that of Augustine. Perhaps the main difference between them is rhetorical. Aquinas, a more systematic and academic theologian than Augustine, was less interested in the personal and pastoral implications of the doctrine than Augustine had been. Both Augustine and Aquinas can be characterized as advocates of single predestination, if by that we mean that they emphasized God's active role in destining some for salvation. Yet they both accepted the idea of reprobation as well. In so doing, they recognized a kind of negative implication of predestination. They thought of reprobation as passive, however, in that it takes the form of a privation.

The reprobate is one whom God leaves to his/her sin. Even more than Augustine, Aquinas developed a complex "compatibilist" philosophy of human agency in order to clarify how it is possible for human intentions and actions to play a significant, if secondary, role in the explanation of the events of history, while God's plan and actions remain the most significant, and primary. Aquinas argued that human agents who act voluntarily, and out of their own internal powers (such as their intellects and wills), have "self-mastery" enough to receive credit and blame for their actions and character traits. I develop these claims about Aquinas's view while offering a reading of his account of Christ's human nature, which he considered both free and predestined.

Chapter four takes up the thought of two Protestants, Luther and Calvin, who are central to many discussions of predestination. Luther's interest in the doctrine was deeply personal, because for him the idea of predestination sums up the Gospel by highlighting the nature of God's favor as an undeserved gift. This emphasis was quite different from the teaching he saw in the church of his day, which misled believers into thinking that they needed to earn and even buy off God's grace. He laid the blame for this erroneous teaching partly at the feet of the Aristotelian philosophy so influential in late medieval theology, and as a result he attempted to avoid philosophical speculation and stick to theological basics. Luther's view can be described as a kind of double predestination, but with the caveat that he would not have accepted any difference between single and double predestination. If salvation depends on God's initiative, those whom God does not choose to save are damned, and it is duplicitous to pretend that God does not intend the ultimate destiny of the reprobate just as much as that of the predestined. Luther did, however, venture beyond the earlier Augustinian tradition with his clear embrace of divine determinism. Luther's claim that sinners can be blamed although they are not free has widely been misunderstood but becomes intelligible once we realize that he was offering a deeply Augustinian view, albeit one shorn of some of Augustine and Aquinas's philosophical clarity and complexity.

I conclude this chapter with brief reflections on Calvin, who was not the radical figure he is often made out to be. Rather, he appropriated Luther's views and systematized them. His clarity about his views made Calvin's double predestinarianism and divine determinism particularly obvious, but the differences between him and Luther are mainly a matter of what aspects of their convictions they emphasized more. Notably, Calvin did depart from Luther by developing a more philosophical noncompetitive theory of divine and human agency. In some of his lesser known works, he even sought help from Aristotle in developing his compatibilist account, which depended on a distinction between being determined and being forced. God, he insists, can do the former without doing the latter, and thus without undermining human agency.

Chapter five, the final historical chapter in the book, focuses on Karl Barth's innovative doctrine of election. Barth's view was supralapsarian, meaning that he thought that God elected Christ prior to anything else. This means that creation is for the sake of Christ, and in order to make Christ possible. The incarnation is, therefore, not primarily a response to sin but valuable for its own sake. Barth developed this view with the further claim that God not only elects Jesus Christ first and above all, but also that God destines him to be both elect and damned, for our sake. This alteration to the traditional doctrine that individual human beings are the primary referent of the decrees concerning salvation made before the creation of the world brings with it a number of possibilities and questions. I first take up some questions about the conceptual and ontological primacy of Jesus, on Barth' view, and then turn to the issue of what it means for human agency to say that all of humanity is elect in Christ. Since Barth contended that the divine decree cannot finally be resisted, there is a deterministic element to his view, though not one that is causal or mechanistic. Barth's insistence on the lack of competition between human and divine agency is tied, in part, to his commitment to the idea that freedom is not tied to having choices but to the ability to obey the divine command that leads to life. This naturally raises the question of whether all are or will be saved. I argue that Barth's theological convictions led him to hope for universal salvation. He could not, however, propound a doctrine of universal salvation because he was uncertain about how such a thing could come to pass.

In the final chapter, I offer a moderate defense of a minimal doctrine of predestination. The doctrine I defend is minimal in that it avoids taking a stand on a number of controversial topics, including determinism and whether one should be committed to universal salvation or not. The defense I offer is moderate, in that I do not argue that predestination is true, but rather that theologians should hold views that allow them to be open to the possibility that it is true. I begin my defense by suggesting that we have reasons to hope that God predestines. Hope, as I use the term here, is not the same as belief based on evidence; one can hope for things that may be unlikely, so long as they are not simply irrational. Second, I contend that trust in divine election makes it easier for us to accept realities of human agency that are otherwise hard to face, such as the ways in which important aspects of the meaning of our existence are out of our control. I then offer two arguments against libertarian views of human agency, on the supposition that those who reject libertarianism are likely to become more open to predestination. These arguments are, first, that libertarianism is unduly speculative, and second, that libertarian free will is likely to be rare even if it does exist. Finally, I take up the problem of a predestining God's relation to evil. My main argument is that predestination does not make this problem worse for the theist than it already is. Indeed, universalist approaches to predestination offer theists a way to make powerful and compelling claims about divine goodness.

1

Augustine on the priority of grace

Although Augustine's defense of predestination has been influential for centuries, it has often been controversial, and has been particularly unpopular among modern thinkers. Some of those who appreciate other aspects of Augustine's writings and influence have taken comfort, however, in the thought that this was one of the last things Augustine wrote. His death in 430 AD came just two or three years after he wrote *On the Predestination of the Saints* and *The Gift of Perseverance*, his only books (originally halves of a single longer work) to explicitly focus on predestination. Perhaps with the best of intentions, some of his readers have speculated that this was the work of a burnt-out old man, his best days behind him, soured by a lifetime of theological conflict and the experience of watching the Roman empire fall apart. Rome had fallen to barbarians while he was alive, and his longtime home, the African port city Hippo Regius, was under siege when he died. Perhaps he lost faith in human agency and turned to God's mysterious and arbitrary direction of history for solace?

However well intentioned, this line of thought is mistaken for at least two reasons. First, *On the Predestination of the Saints* and *The Gift of Perseverance* hardly read as the work of a burnt-out or grumpy old man. This point can be extended, in fact, to four of Augustine's latest works—the two texts just mentioned plus *Grace and Free Choice* and *Rebuke and Grace*. Many of Augustine's most famous works were written in a polemical context, sometimes during prolonged arguments with many of the greatest Christian and non-Christian intellectuals of his time. By contrast, these four books were written as advice to friends, in order to help them give pastoral guidance to monks who were disputing among themselves about how Christians should think about eternal salvation. Their questions had arisen as they read some of Augustine's most polemical books, those attacking the Pelagians, a group of Italian religious leaders who, Augustine believed, had wrongly developed a false tension between God's grace and human agency. Augustine's claim was that one must not deny the power or the necessity of God's grace in order to defend human choice. Augustine's arguments with the Pelagians were prompted by the Christian practice of baptizing infants—which raised the question of why infants, who seem innocent, need to be saved by Christ. Augustine's argument, in brief, was that infants are born with original sin, a guilt and corruption of the spirit that they inherit from their parents. This, the Pelagians believed, was unfair—no one can sin, they argued, unless they voluntarily, knowingly choose to do so.[1]

By contrast, many or even most of the monks to whom Augustine wrote in these texts agreed with him that infants need God's grace in order to be cleansed from original sin and in order to be saved. Nevertheless, some of them sympathized with the Pelagian concern that Augustine's doctrine of grace seemed to disrespect human free choice. Surely, they thought, it is only fair for God to give us a choice about whether we want to be his children or not. Lacking such a choice, how can we be rebuked if we fail to obey God? Because of the conceptual affinity with Pelagianism implied by their concern about Augustine's teaching, the view espoused by these monks would come to be known during the Reformation as Semi-Pelagianism. Augustine, however, seems to have considered their concerns to be a pastoral matter among friends, only indirectly a part of the complex political and religious battles he had been fighting with the Pelagians. His tone is warm and friendly; it lacks the rhetorical punches that were common in the works he had written—and was still writing—against the Pelagains. The tone of these books does not support the thesis that Augustine was worn down or bitter.

Second, the suggestion that Augustine's writing about predestination was out of character for him, and perhaps an expression of anger or exhaustion, fails to take seriously the trajectory of Augustine's thought, which naturally pointed him toward the doctrine of predestination. Although it is often claimed that Augustine developed new ideas in his treatises on *Predestination* and *Perseverance*, it is more accurate to say that in these books Augustine offered a summary of the positive views about grace he had taken himself to be defending, sometimes indirectly, in earlier books such as *Against Julian*. In fact, Augustine himself suggested that a doctrine of predestination had been implicit in his thought since he wrote *To Simplician* in 396, a couple of years before writing his *Confessions*. Reading the Bible after his conversion was, Augustine indicated, what led him to think about predestination. By the time he became a bishop he had also come to think of predestination as a corollary of other beliefs that he considered central to the Christian faith. He particularly saw a fit with the belief that human beings are saved by grace, which he took to mean both that we cannot earn our salvation and that God does not owe salvation to anyone.

This second point about the genesis of Augustine's convictions about predestination deserves further discussion, not least because it will help us to understand why Augustine was committed to the doctrine of predestination. It will be helpful to have that in mind before we go on to consider the details of what Augustine taught in his doctrine of predestination and then inquire into how Augustine defended this doctrine against some of the criticisms it engendered in his time as well as ours. So let us now consider how Augustine came to believe in predestination.

1. How Augustine came to believe in predestination

Augustine was not the first Christian to talk about "predestination." As he noted, some of his own intellectual forbearers, beginning with the apostle Paul, used the term long before him. Indeed, what Matthew Levering calls "the primacy of divine agency" was recognized by many Jewish thinkers even before the advent of Christianity.[2] It is wrong, therefore, to suggest that Augustine invented the idea of predestination. He has, however, exerted a tremendous influence on the meaning of the term "predestination." Augustine saw himself as having inherited his idea of predestination from the Christian tradition he encountered in his influential Italian teacher Ambrose and such African teachers as Cyprian—a complicated claim that we will return to in section two, when we consider Augustine's argument that the doctrine is implied by core Christian convictions. At a minimum, we can say with confidence that Augustine was the first philosophical theologian to carefully develop a doctrine of predestination, and to make it a central part of his theology. Every Christian doctrine of predestination since him owes a great deal to his thought, and he has influenced the thinking of many non-Christians as well.

To defend his teaching about predestination, Augustine turned first to scripture.[3] His reading of scripture on this and many other topics has often been challenged, so it can be helpful to remind ourselves that Augustine did not come to scripture with a belief in predestination, seeking to find evidence for that belief in the Bible. Before his turn to the Catholic faith, and even for some time after his conversion, he showed no evidence of such beliefs. Only as he began to ponder the Bible, and especially the writings of the apostle Paul, did Augustine himself move toward a belief in predestination.

Scripture, Augustine came to believe, teaches predestination both explicitly and implicitly. Predestination is taught explicitly in passages such as the one where Paul straightforwardly states that "those God foreknew he also predestined" (Rom 8; cf. Eph 1:3–5). This all-important discussion suggests not merely that God has foreknowledge of events to come, but also that God has an intentional hand in directing those events, so that some things come to pass precisely because they are part of God's plan. Paul indicates that among those events are the eternal destinies of those who are "elected" by God from the foundation of the world.

Augustine was not only influenced by Paul's writings, however. As we will see, he was also deeply influenced by the idea that Jesus Christ is the first of God's elect, a claim made in a number of New Testament books not written by Paul. In particular, Luke indicates in the Acts of the Apostles that Peter and John considered the events of Jesus' life predested (Acts 4:28). Peter's first letter echoes this claim with the suggestion that Jesus "was chosen before the creation of the world" (1Pet 1:20; cf. Rom 1:1–4, Eph 3:11). The main lines of Augustine's teachings about predestination were based on a fairly straightforward reading of these New Testament writings.

Significantly, however, the texts Augustine referred to most often in his late writings were not passages that specifically mention predestination, but texts that make theological claims that Augustine thought were best explained by a doctrine of predestination.[4] Scripture speaks of divine sovereignty in many passages; of God working things out in accord with the divine plan (e.g., Is 37:29, Prov 16:4). While Augustine believed in a general divine providence by which God does not leave creation alone but is at work within human history, he came to believe something more: that God was not blindsided by what came to pass in creation. Rather, God has always known how this world would turn out. In particular, God always knew that sin and evil would enter the world, but also always intended to respond to those problems through the gift of Jesus Christ, in whom the world is not only healed from its ills but also brought into God's very own life. The ultimate act of divine sovereignty, then, is God having taken evil into account from the beginning via the plan and activity summarized by the term "predestination." As a result, the story of the world is one that God tells, with and through us, though not in such a way as to undermine the significance of our agency (a topic I turn to in greater detail toward the end of this chapter). A classic biblical expression of this two-sided claim about the congruence of human and divine agency is Paul's charge to "continue to work out your salvation with fear and trembling, for it is God who works in you to will and to act according to his good purpose" (Phil 2:12–13).

In developing the doctrine of grace that he considered central to divine predestination, Augustine often referred to a claim made by Jesus: "Without me you can do nothing" (Jn 15:5). This was a theme in Augustine's writing from a fairly early point in his career as a bishop. In fact, Augustine inadvertently started the Pelagian debates by, in his *Confessions*, repeatedly echoing Cyprian's quotation of Paul's rhetorical question "What do you have that you have not received?" (1 Cor 4:7). The Pelagians saw this question as subtly undermining the importance of human agency, by undermining the idea of human autonomy that they considered essential to human freedom. They preferred to emphasize that as free agents we contribute things to the world that are entirely our own. Augustine, by contrast, began more and more to focus on the idea that human agency is secondary, derivative on the powers that make us—God in particular. Thus, he often wrote that we have nothing that we have not received from God. This, he believed, is an idea to which Christians pay homage each time they say the Lord's prayer, and ask not to be brought into temptation but to be given holiness as a gift from God.

Ultimately, Augustine believed that the logic of grace was what pushed him toward a doctrine of predestination. God not only creates us in the first place; God re-creates us by grace once we fall into sin and evil. If we owe everything to God, Augustine reasoned, the doctrine of predestination is an essential part of an explanation of how and why that is so. The doctrine expresses the trust that the trajectory of our lives lie within the divine plan, rather than simply being events that God reacts to and attempts to make meaning out of after the fact. Faith, Augustine insisted, is a gift of God, not something we can earn: "It is, of course, not grace if any merits come before it, for what is given, not as grace, but as something due, is a repayment for merits rather than a gift."[5]

We have begun to see why Augustine thought that even in places where the Bible does not explicitly mention the idea of predestination, the concept is at work. We can see as well that this claim is not only an assertion about the logic of the divine economy of grace but also a biographical reference. Augustine himself appears to have first begun to ponder the meaning of biblical claims about the divine economy when, reading the book of *Romans*, he was struck by St. Paul's reference to the ancient story of Jacob and Esau, who were twins and for much of their lives, rivals. In later scriptural reflection on that story a prophet writes, speaking from God's point of view, that "Jacob I loved but Esau I hated" (Rom 9:13, citing Mal 1:2–3). This love that God has for Jacob (who God elects to become one of the great forefathers of Israel) is bestowed even before Jacob or Esau are born, Augustine noted. The election of Jacob to carry God's favor, including the promises made to Abraham, therefore appeared to be prior to any merits with which Jacob might have been able to earn God's favor. To use a theological term that has become common in descriptions of this Augustinian idea, Augustine thought of God's love, and God's grace, as *prevenient*, "coming before." God's grace is always prior to our merits, and any sense in which God recognizes our merits and responds to them with favor is secondary.

An obvious reply to the inferences Augustine drew from this story (a reply Augustine heard in his own day, and for a time believed himself) is that God must have chosen Jacob because God foreknew that Jacob would trust in him and be obedient in ways that his brother Esau was not. If so, Jacob's future merits (compared to Esau's future demerits) would provide a basis on which Jacob could have been preferred. However, Augustine saw no reason to think that this view is supported by the biblical text. On the contrary, he found it opposed to the point scripture seemed to be making, which is precisely that the initiative lay with God.

Augustine also offered a philosophical counterargument built on this exegetical point. If God did run things by taking into account counterfactual events that have not actually happened, it would make nonsense of many aspects of the Christian life.[6] For instance, Augustine wondered whether God would have to reward or punish people for what they would have done had they not died. At the least, it is problematic to reward people ahead of time for doing things that they have not done yet; that undermines the importance of actually doing specific things. From a theological point of view, the most worrisome implication of the idea that God preferred Jacob for what Jacob was later going to do, Augustine wrote, is that it implies that Jesus Christ did not actually have to have become incarnate in order for him to be the savior. Jesus could have saved the human race even before he was born! But, of course, that is clearly not how the Christian tradition has thought about the effects of Jesus' life and death. Therefore, Augustine reasoned, it could not have been true that God worked that way with regard to Jacob. He found it far less problematic to believe that God destined Jacob for greatness, and empowered him to become who he came to be.

It took a couple of decades for Augustine to fully apply the ideas he had about heroes of the faith like Jacob being predestined by God to the rest of the race. Eventually, he came to think that although Jacob was in many ways a unique figure, he was also uniquely representative of those who became part of his heritage in Israel and later the church. Like him, they too were predestined by God, saved by grace rather than their own efforts. This is a view that Augustine only wrote about explicitly in his late works, near the end of his life. It took quite a while for Augustine to fully develop the conclusions about grace and predestination that he wrote about near the end of his life, perhaps because he himself was uncertain about the implications of these views, and how to defend them without falling into fatalism. It may be helpful for us to remember that Augustine's career as an author was not his only or even, at many points, his main occupation. He was a leader in his home city, the African church, and active in Roman politics as well. It would not be surprising, then, if even so brilliant a figure as St. Augustine were to have found it difficult to attend to the full implications of some of his own thoughts and insights, at least for a time.

Looking back over his life, however, Augustine argued that there had been a fundamental consistency in his thought, which focused on the inability to save oneself and the necessity of being dependent on God's healing work through Christ.[7] Doubtless for rhetorical purposes, while at the same time offering a plausible description of his own intellectual trajectory, he maintained that his ideas about predestination were implicit in much of his writing. Augustine saw predestination as a corollary of his long-held view that although our agency is an important part of the world's story it is most fundamentally God who shapes our identities, and who founds our dignity. Augustine repeatedly warned against pride—the sin, he believed, of his Donatist and Pelagian opponents—because thinking too much of yourself not only misunderstands what it means to be human but also denies the goodness of God, and reveals confusion about how our world is structured.

Belief in predestination was, for Augustine, based on a core conviction that he emphasized and developed more as his career progressed—the claim that we find the help we need only in Christ. If it is really true that without him we are lost, the significant corollary is that our agency is limited in important ways; we cannot make anything we might wish of ourselves. We can, however, really be what God calls us to be when God gives us the strength. Behind Augustine's doctrine of predestination, therefore, lay an analysis of the nature and limits of human agency, and of how our agency fits with God's. Before discussing that point further, however, it will be helpful to have before us a more detailed account of Augustine's concept of predestination.

2. The content of Augustine's doctrine of predestination

We have seen, somewhat briefly, that the Bible, and the Christian tradition even prior to Augustine, speaks of predestination and closely related ideas. However, the meaning of the term took on a very particular cast in Augustine's hands—and as we will see, not all of the theologians who came after Augustine meant the same by predestination as he did. This is true even for theologians who owed a great deal to Augustine's teaching. It is important, therefore, to consider with care the particular content of Augustine's doctrine of predestination.

This task is made more challenging by the fact that Augustine's own views were in progress during the course of his career.[8] Because he was the first to try to think systematically through the implications of what we now call Augustinian doctrines of grace, freedom, and predestination, there are a number of ways in which his views are not as clearly developed as the views of those who came after him, and who were able to build on the beginnings Augustine made (Aquinas will be our example of this point, in chapter 3). Augustine did not, for instance, have at his disposal the distinction between single and double predestination. It can be difficult, therefore, to ascertain which camp he would have subscribed to, had he been asked—or even if he would have chosen a side rather than coming up with some other brilliant approach of his own! Nevertheless, it is possible to trace the implications of the claims Augustine did and did not make, and we will see that many things can be inferred about Augustine's doctrine of predestination once we have done so. At the same time, we must keep in mind that attempts to place Augustine in relation to theological developments of the doctrine of predestination that came after him necessarily remain somewhat speculative.

It may be easier to understand what Augustine had in mind when he wrote about predestination if we start by considering his two favorite models of predestination: infants who were involuntarily baptized into union with Christ, and Christ himself.[9] Focusing first on Christ will help us to then understand an analogy Augustine sought to make between adults and infants.

It is notable that Augustine spoke not merely of predestination, as if that were some generic act or power that God has, but of the predestination of the saints. The predestination of the saints, Augustine wrote, "is nothing other than the foreknowledge and the preparation of the benefits of God by which he most certainly sets free whoever are set free."[10] Predestination is, therefore, a special relationship that God has with select persons God elects to save.

The fact that Augustine saw a connection between predestination and setting free makes it particularly interesting that Augustine emphasized that "the predestination of the saints...was seen most clearly in the Holy One of all holy ones," the pure Son of God who was also an Israelite first son, in the line of David.[11] He was concerned enough about this point that he discussed it three separate times in his books on *Predestination* and *Perseverance*. He went so far as to end the latter work with a reminder that Christ is the model of predestination. Yet when we apply Augustine's definition of predestination to Christ, it might seem somewhat odd. Why is there a need for Jesus, the second person of the Trinity incarnate in human flesh, to be set free? Is he not, as God, always completely free? And how can God be predestined?

Augustine undoubtedly considered the Son, the second person of the Trinity, fully and forever free; indeed, the Son sets free. Likewise, as God, the Son predestines; the Son was not predestined. God could not predestine one who already existed, who was very God, who already had a nature and character and had oriented himself toward the world in love. Thus, when Augustine expanded upon the scriptural claim that Jesus Christ is predestined for service by God, he had in mind the traditional theological idea that the one historical person, Jesus, has two natures.[12] One of these natures, the Son, is divine, and cannot be predestined or set free by God's action. The other nature, however, is a human nature. Unlike the Son, who is eternal, the human nature of Christ comes into being when Jesus is conceived by Mary. This human nature is predestined, chosen by God out of all the other possibilities God might have bestowed this honor upon, and given the entirely undeserved blessing of being united with the Son as the human nature of Jesus Christ.

In spite of its unique status, Augustine understood Jesus' human nature as the paradigmatic example of those about whom Jesus said "You have not chosen me, but I have chosen you."[13] As we have seen, this is true of all the human beings God relates to, but this general truth is modeled more dramatically by some human beings than others. Jacob is one particularly important example, as are the children of Israel collectively. More than any of these others, however, Jesus' human nature is elevated to the greatest heights. Jesus' human nature was not made part of the incarnation because it was deserving, or because it would come to merit its elevation. Rather, it was selected by grace to become a vehicle of divine loving kindness.

It was not in a position to earn such honor, in part because such a great honor—being made part of God's own self—is a kind of honor that can only be bestowed, not earned. Nothing it could have done, had it lived its own separate life, could have warranted such favor. Yet although the favor that Christ's human nature was granted was, of course, singular, Augustine saw something typical of God's action in the world in this act of gracious condescension:

> He, therefore, who made Christ a righteous man...a man who was never not righteous, without any preceding merits of his will, makes righteous persons from unrighteous ones without any preceding merits of their will in order that Christ might be the head and they might be his members.[14]

God elects, from the beginning, to make Christ's human nature righteous. God does so not because it is deserved but so that it can have a role in doing the work God seeks to do. This exemplifies the logic of predestination, the saving grace God gives to many. Thus, Christ's human nature is the paradigm of predestination.

It might still be unclear how Christ's human nature is, as Augustine indicated in his definition of predestination, set free by God's election of it for participation in Christ. There are two potential sources of confusion here. The first is that Christ's human nature is not corrupted by sin, and is therefore never in bondage. It therefore seems not to need to be freed by God. A second confusion is with Augustine's use of the term freedom in this context. Predestination, after all, involves a divine determination that human beings are unable to gainsay. What God predestines must come to pass. If we think of freedom as a kind of autonomy, it will seem that Jesus' human nature does indeed lack freedom, precisely because it is predestined to be part of the second person of the Trinity, and to be perfect in the ways that are suitable for Christ to be. It is not given a choice in the matter.

These puzzles are resolved once we recognize that Augustine did not think of freedom in the libertarian manner that has become typical in our time. For Augustine, freedom is not the ability to have or actualize unconstrained choices but the ability to fulfill one's nature, and to be fulfilled as a person. Since human beings are relational, made to live in communities of love, human beings are fully free when they not only are able to live in love but are actually doing so. As Augustine famously wrote in his *Confessions*, our hearts are restless until they find rest in God's embrace, which draws us not only into the divine life of the Father, Son, and Spirit but also into the life of God's family, the church. Divine predestination bestows freedom, therefore, by bestowing a power to love well, and fulfillment of that love in actual relationships. The better and more full the relationships, the more free a person is. That is why even Christ's unfallen human nature can be made free by the gracious empowerment of God. For Augustine, freedom is normative—it is living in the manner God made us to live, and has always planned for the saints to live.

If thinking about freedom in this manner seems strange, it might be helpful to think about some analogies. Consider, for instance, the fact that most people love surprises. When they receive a surprise gift, or a surprise party, an essential part of their delight in those things is the fact that they did not choose them, but someone who cares about them chose for them, with their best interests in mind. Their pleasure in the surprise is, of course, mitigated if the gift is poorly chosen, but this does not necessarily mean they are shallow, and only interested in getting what they want. Rather, they may be crestfallen because they believed their friends knew them better. The freedom for loving relationships that Augustine had in mind is like a surprise gift that fits you perfectly, because it is given by a friend who knows you supremely well. It might not have been what you would have picked out for yourself; perhaps you thought that it would make you happy if people would just leave you alone, or perhaps you thought that you knew what sort of people you would prefer to associate with. Once you have received the gift, however, you know that it was a better gift than you could have found on your own, had you looked for yourself. The fittingness of the gift matters more, in such a case, than your being able to choose it, and you can delight in the gift because it is good. This is how the relationship between divine and human freedom works, from Augustine's perspective.

Of course, the analogy is imperfect. In the case of predestination, the gift that is given is not merely some add-on to one's life; it is a new life. The gift of salvation that God gives is one's own self, renewed. Thus, it is a much more serious affair than an everyday birthday gift. The gift in question is, perhaps, more like the sort of gift parents give their children if they are faithful as parents and committed to the long process of formation that is required for a child to develop the ability to speak, read, properly process emotions, and so on. These are not goods a child could ask for or know to seek; they must be bestowed. When they are bestowed rightly they conduce to the child's freedom, enhancing her or his agency rather than detracting from it.

Augustine would have taken this point to be in his favor, precisely because he was concerned about the fact that even in the case of adults the gift that God gives is a new way of being oneself, a truer and better way of being than one could have imagined on one's own. Augustine believed that we are unable to give each other, or ourselves, such gifts. So it is not as though God could have taken a step back and asked us what we wanted, or waited for us to make it happen of our own accord. Like children, we simply do not know what to ask, or what to look for. If we are to have the highest freedom, Augustine thought, it must be bestowed on us by the one who made us in the first place.

In this life, in a fallen world, it makes sense that freedom is often thought to depend on our having unconstrained choices. Since there are many corrupt yet powerful people around us, our loves are able to be fulfilled only if we have leeway to pursue them. We sometimes feel that no one is watching out for us except ourselves, and there is enough truth in this notion that it offers us a genuine motive for wanting government as well as other forces to leave us to our own devices, rather than attempting to coopt us. A political freedom of choice is a genuine good in such a context, one that Augustine affirmed, within certain limitations. Augustine always kept in mind, however, that political freedom of choice is a penultimate freedom. He was not confident that we know ourselves and our good well enough for our choices to ultimately serve us well. Human agents are fallible and should, therefore, hold back when they can. However, it is better for us when God directs our paths. That is where our deeper freedom lies—not in being self-made but in being who God meant us to be from the beginning. Our way of being good was not merely foreseen by God at the foundation of the world but planned by God as part of the reason for making this world in the first place.

Having come this far, we are in a position to understand why Augustine thought of infant baptism as providing a second paradigm for thinking about predestination. When we think about

adults we quite easily make the mistake of thinking that they
are, or at least can be, self-made. Adult human beings are centers
of significant power. They often seem capable of directing their
own stories, and in many ways they do. It is misleading, however,
to contemplate the agency of an adult without thinking about
that person's history. Whatever knowledge, rational capacities,
desires, volitional capacities, and so on an adult human person
might have are gifts, not simply of the creator who endowed
that person with them, but of the other people and societies who
upheld the life of the child who became that man or woman.
What they have, they have received. As we grow into adulthood
we are tempted to forget how dependent, how communal we are;
thinking that you can make it on your own is one insidious form
that pride takes. These features of human existence are harder to
ignore when we focus on infants, however, and that was one of
the reasons Augustine was interested in them.

Augustine argued that the widespread Christian practice of baptizing infants even before infants are capable of comprehending
what such a sacrament might mean is a practice that lays bare the
reality that "every claim to human merits preceding the grace of
God collapses."[15] In baptism, which (as Augustine liked to remind
his readers) the Nicene creed recognizes as a blessing given for
the forgiveness of sins, infants are given a grace they did not seek,
let alone earn. In this they are like Jacob and Jesus, who were elected
by God before they were.

Of course, there are some significant differences between adults
and infants. One, relevant for our purposes, is that although baptism is part of God's providence, it is not a sure sign of predestination. After all, predestination is God's decision to bestow upon a
person that perfect freedom that is available only to those who have
been unified with the Son, through Christ. Baptism does, Augustine
believed, draw infants into Christ, but this drawing is uncertain and
incomplete. Some who are baptized can be lost, unless they receive
further grace, particularly including the grace Augustine came to
call perseverance. Unlike the election of Jesus' human nature, infant
baptism, therefore, is not an example of predestination. Rather, it
is an example of the logic of predestination, the idea that God's
grace is prevenient. Those who are committed to infant baptism,
Augustine believed, should also be committed to a doctrine of
predestination, and for the same theological reasons. As we will

see, Augustine made a similar argument about those who believe in divine foreknowledge: those who believe in one should believe in both. But belief in infant baptism does not commit one to also believing in predestination—a point Augustine could have made more carefully had it suited his purposes to do so.

For Augustine, there is no sure sign of predestination that is discernible to the human eye or heart. Predestination is a decision God has made to save, but a person could go on for many years without hearing God's call (as Augustine himself had). Even after being baptized, one cannot ascertain whether one is predestined, whether by looking inside oneself or by judging one's works. Not everyone who is given the grace to seek God, or who shows signs of being sanctified by God's love, is one of God's elect. That is because God does not give all graces to all people. Some are empowered by God in ways that fall short of bringing them all the way to eternal salvation—and when asked why that is so Augustine could only bow before the inscrutability of what he believed were God's judgments. Those who are given the grace of perseverance are marked in just one way: they all kept their faith in Christ until the end of their days.[16] But as I have already indicated, Augustine did not believe that there was any straightforward way to tell who had indeed kept the faith until the end, or whether he himself had. Beyond that Augustine did not inquire; uncertainty is part of this life, but one should always seek God to the best of one's ability.

Augustine certainly recognized that one could raise the questions about "assurance" of salvation that would become a major concern for doctrines of predestination after the Reformation. However, Augustine seems neither to have had such concerns himself nor to have found concerns about assurance to be a major aspect of his pastoral ministry—although he did encourage preachers not to remind the members of their churches that they may not be predestined; nothing good can come of that! On the whole, Augustine seems to have taken an attitude similar to the one Luther would later defend: when we ask whether God loves us, we should turn to the testimonies God has given us in scripture and in the sacraments. In particular, we should turn to Christ, and seek God in our prayers: "heaven forbid that you despair about yourselves, because you are commanded to place your hope in him, not in yourselves."[17] Augustine's doctrine of predestination, then, teaches about who we are in relation to God, but it was not meant for us to cling to if we seek personal reassurance of our relationship with God.

One further clarification about Augustine's doctrine of predestination may be worth venturing, before we pursue more fully his explanation of how predestination does not undermine human agency. While Augustine was not aware of the distinction between single and double predestination that would later develop, it seems most appropriate to read Augustine as committed to the idea of single predestination. The evidence for this is the fact that he always spoke of predestination as an expression of divine love. Indeed, we have seen that he focused on examples of predestination that are positive—predestination is always to heaven—and he defined predestination as grace.

Having said that, an obvious question arises. Augustine certainly did not believe that those who are not predestined are able to be saved. Only by grace are we saved. No one can save her or himself. Thus, those who are not chosen by God will necessarily go to hell. It might seem, therefore, that Augustine must have been committed to double predestination. As we will see, this is a complex issue mainly because the distinction between double and single predestination is fraught with ambiguity. For now, it is helpful to use the idea of single predestination to remind ourselves that Augustine thought of predestination as an act of grace. In addition, Augustine did not believe that the fall into sin or damnation is effected by God's direct activity. Rather, these are events that God permits. Having said that, we should also note that although Augustine found it natural that the Bible speaks of both human and angelic persons being damned to hell, he also questioned why God would help some people, while allowing others to be trapped by sin and not given aid. On the one hand, he acknowledged that he had no answer to the question of why God saves some specific persons and not others. That decision is a mystery, he affirmed. On the other hand, however, Augustine speculated that God may allow some to fall away so that those who are saved will be all the more aware of God's grace, and how it differs from God's justice.[18] This defense of God's plan might seem weak to us, but it is worth keeping in mind that Augustine did not believe in hell mainly because he thought it made conceptual sense. Rather, he was committed to it because he considered it an article of the Christian faith, clearly taught by scripture. He believed God in order to understand the content of the faith, but he was aware that he did not always understand very much, or very well.

I mentioned early in this chapter that Augustine also claimed that his doctrine of predestination was nothing new: the revered Christian teachers Ambrose and Cyprian had already taught these ideas before him. Having seen what Augustine believed about predestination, we can now assess the sense in which he was right. Augustine had indeed learned from Ambrose and Cyprian about the priority of God's grace, about God's sovereignty, and about divine foreknowledge. It was an exaggeration, however, for Augustine to claim that his teachers' claims about prevenience amounted to doctrines of predestination. So while he did maintain continuity with the tradition that preceded him, Augustine also added to it. We will see that he was not the last to do so!

3. Predestination and human agency

Many of St. Augustine's contemporaries sympathized with the theological commitments that drove him to his doctrine of predestination. Undoubtedly, his eloquence in expressing the gospel of grace and his dogged attempts to apply the implications of that gospel to every aspect of life were significant reasons why he was so widely recognized as a great teacher and leader. Many of his contemporaries accepted and defended his claims about original sin, infant baptism, salvation through Christ alone, and predestination. The Pelagians, of course, did not accept the first and last of these claims, and as a result they understood the meaning of the second and third claims quite differently from Augustine. But this was a rhetorical, conceptual, and political battle the Pelagians lost, at least for a while; too many of Augustine's contemporaries were on his side, or came over to it.

Even so, some found it troubling that Augustine had extended his claims about the priority of grace so far, and so openly. Some cautioned that even if the doctrine of predestination he was preaching was true, it would be better to keep quiet about it. It was more strategic, they argued, for Christians to focus on other teachings that were not likely to incentivize laziness on the part of Christians who might too casually take for granted that they were among God's elect, and thus needed to do nothing more, or to drive to despair those who might fear they had not been selected by God for eternal happiness. In a word, they feared either that the doctrine of predestination had fatalistic implications, or that it was too hard to explain why the doctrine does not. Either way, the best approach was to keep the doctrine unpublicized.

Augustine's response to these concerns can be classified under three main points. First, as we have seen, he reminded his conversation partners that the doctrine is true, a central Christian belief that is taught in the scripture. If it is part of the gospel, it should be preached. Indeed, Augustine believed that it had been preached, if only indirectly. Second, we have also seen that Augustine considered the doctrine of predestination to be central to a proper understanding of what God is up to in giving us Jesus Christ. Not least, it helped make sense of the practice of infant baptism. "Predestination," Augustine wrote, "must be preached in order that the genuine grace of God...grace which is not given according to our merits, can be defended by an insurmountable bulwark."[19] Third, it has sometimes been forgotten that Augustine believed that he could offer a philosophical defense explaining why and how it was less problematic to adhere to a doctrine of predestination than some of his friends and allies believed. This is the claim we will focus on in this section.

There are actually two parts to Augustine's philosophical defense of predestination. Both, in different ways, engage the worry that predestination makes human beings responsible for too little as well as the worry that predestination makes God responsible for too much. The first part of Augustine's defense against these fears is his claim that believing in predestination does not have implications any more problematic than other beliefs to which Christians are widely committed. Augustine singles out the common Christian belief in divine foreknowledge to make his point (and I will argue in the final chapter of this book that it is not the only doctrine he could have chosen).

Augustine's argument is as follows.[20] The problem with predestination is supposed to be that it leads to fatalism.[21] That is, it leads us to give up on the significance of our agency because it teaches us that God is the one making the important decisions about how each of our stories will play out. It is often suggested that this is a uniquely problematic doctrine. But, Augustine noted, predestination is not the only Christian teaching that gives the impression of making human effort and planning seem pointless. He might have mentioned his doctrine of original sin, but since that was a contested teaching he focused on a doctrine that was very widely accepted—the idea that God has foreknowledge of all future events. Even by Augustine's time it had become clear that the doctrine of divine foreknowledge raises questions similar to those raised by his doctrine of predestination.

If God foreknows that I will eat too much molten chocolate ecstasy cake tomorrow, it might seem pointless to rebuke me for it. After all, I did not have an alternative to doing so. Afterwards, even once it is true that I have overeaten, I can say in my defense that I am the sort of person who does that sort of thing because God foreknew that I would. I can say, in short, that it was necessary for me to overeat, and that because of God's foreknowledge I had no choice in the matter. In making this point, Augustine was not accepting that Christianity is fatalistic. Rather, he was making a comparative point: if he is supposed to give up on divine predestination because it invites laziness on the part of Christian believers, it looks as though he would also have to give up on divine foreknowledge. But that, he assumed, is not palatable to Christians, whose belief in God's promises would be shaken if the future were opaque to God.[22] And if Christians can remain committed to the doctrine of divine foreknowledge in spite of the questions it raises about the manner in which our agency relates to God's, Augustine thought his interlocutors could hold on to the doctrine of predestination as well. Another way of putting this point would be as follows: Augustine's claim is that his belief in predestination did not add anything uniquely philosophically problematic to Christian belief. Commitment to divine sovereignty had already raised the relevant questions. Thus, if the problem with the doctrine of predestination is supposed to be that it does not allow us to have undetermined choices, Augustine addressed this problem, in part, by arguing that this is a problem that Christians who believe in divine foreknowledge already face.

It is important to be clear about the fact that Augustine considered fatalism absurd. He did not believe that our decisions or actions count for nothing, or that we can simply credit God with making us pursue whatever goods or evils we find appealing. God is not the only significant agent in Augustine's universe. Thus, the point of his reminder that belief in divine foreknowledge can lead to fatalism is not that since Christians have already given up on human agency they might as well accept the doctrine of predestination too. Rather, his point was that Christians cannot escape fatalism simply by jettisoning belief in predestination. Instead, they should develop a theory of human agency that allows them to understand how it is possible for the necessities involved in divine foreknowledge and predestination to be compatible with meaningful human agency. Predestination and foreknowledge might imply that we lack alternatives to being who we are, but this, Augustine maintained, does not mean that we are not free or responsible agents.

This leads us to the second part of Augustine's philosophical defense of predestination, the noncompetitive conceptions of agency and freedom he developed in his writings against the Pelagians, and put to work in his books against the "semi-Pelagians." We have already seen that Augustine's conception of freedom differs from the libertarian understanding widely taken for granted in our time, which associates freedom with having choices. Because many of Augustine's readers assume that freedom must mean the ability to make nonnecessary choices among alternatives, it has often been said that Augustine gives up on freedom in his late work.[23] Augustine, however, disputed such charges—he was not giving up on freedom itself, but rather on a particular conception of freedom. It is not sufficient, therefore, to charge Augustine with a lack of interest in freedom; we must engage him in a discussion of the kinds of freedom there are, and which of those are worth having. Here, I offer an introductory discussion of Augustine's views that seeks to make his concerns, which are commonly misunderstood, intelligible to modern readers.[24]

Augustine had what analytic philosophers call a "compatibilist" conception of freedom and of human responsibility, meaning that these goods are compatible with divine determinations such as predestination. As Augustine put it, "...if necessity is defined in the sense according to which we say that it is necessary for something to be as it is or to happen as it does, I see no reason to fear that it will eliminate our freedom of will."[25]

In this book, I use the idea that human and divine agencies are "non-competitive" as a synonym for the idea that they are compatible. Our agency is not in competition with God's because the two are compatible; God is the primary cause and we are secondary. These terms are helpful markers, but their meaning must be developed if they are to genuinely help us understand Augustine's views. The crucial question is—how can our agency remain genuine and significant if God is the primary author of our stories? If we are not able to reject God's direction, then in what sense do we remain responsible for our own narrative arcs?

Augustine was up front about the fact that, on his view, the grace God offers to his predestined elect is necessarily accepted by those to whom it is given.[26] Augustine also maintained that God does not cause us to act sinfully.[27] Thus, divine predestination creates only a positive kind of necessity, one that fulfills the ends for which God made us (again, Augustine subscribed to single, not double, predestination). And although it is clear that this "blessed necessity" will, at least at times, take choice away from human beings, Augustine was eager to affirm that it does not remove the ability to act voluntarily.

Augustine offered a picture of human agency to explain how this is possible. Fundamentally, he believed, human beings are not autonomous masters of their fates but dependent, spiritually hungry beings who (whether we know it or not) yearn for a relationship with God, and with the goods through which God displays his glory. When we act or speak we do so for reasons; we are motivated to do so by the concerns and beliefs we have. To put the point another way, the decisions we make are informed by what we find attractive, and what we consider true. Augustine liked to remind his readers that, as Ambrose had said, what comes into our thoughts and rises up in our hearts is not in our power to control— not directly, at least. This means that we have limited control over our character, which comprises the things we think about, or do not care to think about, and what we do or do not desire. Moreover, if we have limited control over the virtues and vices that characterize us, we have limited control over what we say and do, because what we say and do flows from our character. Our lack of control over ourselves is one of the reasons why we cannot become more virtuous without divine help.

Augustine is sometimes misread on this point. He did not mean to suggest that everything we say or do is predetermined. It is true that God has oversight over all creation; as Augustine argued at length in *City of God*, human kingdoms are established by divine providence. But that does not imply that God directs every little detail of creation's existence. In fact, Augustine argued, "[God] is not the giver of all wills."[28] There are many times when God simply allows us to do as we please. Adam and Eve's fall from perfection into sin is the clearest example of such a situation, where God foreknew a thing that God did not cause.[29]

In addition, Augustine left open the possibility that there are times when we make undetermined choices. There will be times when we do not find anything attractive enough that it trumps our other options. We may, for example, choose to eat whatever we happen to see first as we look into the refrigerator, or whatever comes to mind first as we try to figure out what to get for takeout. There is nothing necessary about such events. However, he was convinced that indeterminacy of this sort is far from constituting the essence of our agency. Augustine argued that we most fully realize ourselves when we are able to pursue a good wholeheartedly, doing what we want for our reasons, without the internal division that choice bespeaks. In fact, as our discussion of God's normative freedom implied, he considered the highest kind of freedom to be an inability to love wrongly that did not leave room for choice.

Inspired both by the scripture and neo-Platonic themes, Augustine often used romantic metaphors to express his understanding of our search for God and God's goodness in this life. Appropriating those metaphors, which we still use in ways not unlike Augustine's, may help us understand his view better. If the Christian life is like a great romance, in which God is courting us and we are—whether we know it or not—seeking the thrill of whatever hints of God's company we can find, Augustine's hope was not to be undecided about where to commit his love. If he were able to hold back in such a way, weighing his options, it would suggest that none of the candidates for his hands were really eminently suitable for him. But having found his perfect match in God, Augustine believed it did not speak well of him when he did hold back; his best moments were when he was fully "into" the relationship. As long as the relationship was the perfect fit, Augustine saw no reason for him to want to have a choice about it. He was happy to be carried away.

Centuries later, John Dunne expressed Augustine's view beautifully in a famous and controversial sonnet:

Batter my heart, three-person'd God; for you
As yet but knock; breathe, shine, and seek to mend;
That I may rise, and stand, o'erthrow me, and bend
Your force, to break, blow, burn, and make me new.

I, like an usurp'd town, to another due,
Labour to admit you, but O, to no end.
Reason, your viceroy in me, me should defend,
But is captiv'd, and proves weak or untrue.
Yet dearly I love you, and would be loved fain,
But am betroth'd unto your enemy;
Divorce me, untie, or break that knot again,
Take me to you, imprison me, for I,
Except you enthrall me, never shall be free,
Nor ever chaste, except you ravish me.[30]

Augustine did not think, as Dunne's sonnet has sometimes been thought to imply, that God's grace does violence, or forces itself upon his beloved. As Dunne actually suggests, this is a ravishing that is sought by the beloved, who hopes to receive a new heart, one that will not have divided loyalties. Divorce from evil is a kind of healing. This language of romantic passion might become problematic if it were a notion of losing oneself in God, but Augustine insisted that it is more the case that we find ourselves in God. That is because of the nature of the relationship: to be in Christ is to be healed of your worst problems of heart and mind by the one who made you in the first place. Such a relationship, Augustine believed, is not agency-demeaning but agency-enhancing, if we understand the true nature of our agency rightly. Voluntary agency, which God does not take away from us, is more central to our way of being in the world than having choices. Choice is only a minor good, an occasional means to an end rather than an end in itself. Moreover, whether through choice or whatever other means we are not able to define ourselves, because whatever choices we make are always sourced in our existing way of being in the world. However, when we are blessed by God our voluntary agency is enhanced.

In *City of God* Augustine explained this dynamic by reminding his readers that voluntary agency exists only in those into whom God has breathed the breath of life, which is God's own uncreated spirit.[31] To receive more of that life can only be empowering. Precisely because God empowers by giving the Trinitarian life that is divine, grace is an empowering for the virtues that make it possible for us to live in harmony with others and ourselves. Only when our loves are thus harmonized can we finally pursue what we want.

It is because of these views that, although Augustine was not a determinist (particularly not in our typically Newtonian, mechanistic sense), he did not necessarily consider it problematic to be determined, and to lack choice. In fact, he thought that the solution to sinful unhappiness was to be determined by the right source of love. Thus, from an Augustinian point of view, the agential problem with sinners is not that they are determined, or lack choices, but that they cannot get what they truly want. By loving in the wrong ways at the wrong times sinners put themselves in the position of necessarily being unhappy. They do this because they ask God's good creation to be for them what it is not—an ultimate rather than a finite good. And in their attempts to make it more than it is, they distort the goodness that it does have. In a way, the sinner distorts every good in a manner like the way in which those who support prostitution change the meaning of sex. Money makes sex not an interpersonal expression of love but a narcissistic and epicurean commodity to be consumed. Sinners make a similar mistake when they seek created goods as something other than a beautiful gift that celebrates their relationship with God.

In particular, sinners often want themselves to be more than a gift; they want to deserve God's love, to earn favor, and to be worthy of it. Augustine, however, believed that we must accept the paradox that we both are and are not meritorious, without despairing. In one way, we are not meritorious because every good thing we have has been a gift. We, therefore, cannot fairly credit ourselves with whatever may be wonderful about us because we are characters who have been drawn up by a master storyteller who gave us the qualities we have in order to tell a particular story. When we live, we live out of that story that God is telling; we do not simply create our own scripts. Again, that is not to say that every last thing we do or are is predetermined by God. Augustine's point, rather, is that whatever positive agential resources we have we owe to God, and to those other people God has put in our lives. We are secondary agents because our agency always draws its direction and its power from the things that make us who we are—and Augustine firmly believed that it was foolish to think we can re-make our selves. We must accept that, as images of God, we are derivative.

At the same time, however, we are meritorious because the story that God wishes to tell is a story about God's being in personal relationships. It may be helpful to think back on Augustine's comments about Christ's human nature as the central example of this relationship. Jesus' human nature is not overwhelmed even if it is the secondary figure in the relationship. On the contrary, his agency is enhanced. That is because the manner in which God blesses us is with a unique personal agency. As significant voluntary agents, whose beliefs and desires make a difference, we deserve to be praised and blamed for who we are, and we naturally respond to other people's rebukes or compliments. It matters to others what qualities are shown in our behavior, or lack of behavior, and it matters to us what attitudes others display in response to the qualities that are displayed in our lives. Having the kind of voluntary agency we have, and the abilities to think, dream, wish, and so on that go along with it, means that we are responsible agents, accountable for who we are. Of course, that status, too, is not something we have to or can earn; it is bestowed. Yet it really is bestowed, and it is ours. Created beings are derivative but we also have responsibility for the persons we are. As Augustine wrote, our believing and willing "are due to [God] because he prepares the will, and both are due to us because they are not done unless we are willing."[32]

One analogy that Augustine used to convey this point is that of prayer. Prayer, of course, is a practice central to the Christian life. But as the activity proper to those who wait upon the Lord to renew their strength, it is also a metaphor for the entire Christian life, one that sums up the dynamic Augustine had in mind when he asked, "What do you have that you have not received?"[33] The *Confessions* took the form of an extended prayer because in that book Augustine expressed his sense that his life story, and whatever sense it makes, is due to God's gracious planning. In his prayers he offered a testimony about his reliance on God, but at the same time he displayed his own agency by speaking in his own voice. He was a dependent agent, but not in such a way that he was not a responsible agent in his own right. He spoke for himself, expressing his own beliefs and desires in the manner appropriate to a genuine conversation partner with God, even if that voice was given to him by his maker.

For Augustine, then, the life of prayer is a life of extended testimony about and with God. It is a conversation in which we are subordinate yet still significant partners. We have thoughts and desires of our own, and we can express these to God for our own reasons. As conversation partners with whom God has special, personal, relationships, we are deserving of praise when we are good, and deserving of blame and rebuke when we are evil.

When we are evil we can, however, seem to be in a situation in which we lack agency—a claim that Augustine both endorsed and rejected. He certainly found the agency of sinners lacking in significant respects, and Augustine displayed a good deal of concern for sinners, among whom he placed himself. He acknowledged that in his sin—when he became overly enraptured by some of the goods God made, and this ended up distorting his relationships with God and with the other goods God made, including other people—he had not always known what he was doing. Often he had thought he was making his life better, even when in fact he had been making chains for himself out of the things he had loved, not well. Augustine's problem, caused by the original sin he inherited from his own origins, was both ignorance and weakness. These were problems of relationships, not merely to external goods, such as the admiration of others, but—perhaps most crucially—to himself. His agency was faulty, at best imperfect, because he did not even know himself very well. He had a sense of his wants, his love for love, but he was not really sure what was worth wanting, or what he should orient his life around. Worse, even when he had an idea of what he sought, he was unable to understand his own mind's proclivities. Often, it seemed that even what he believed to be worthwhile he only wanted halfheartedly. A significant part of the problem is that he was divided against himself. Augustine spoke of himself as a person in fragments, not as a person of a single will but of partial loves and wishes. This problem was compounded by the fact that he was unable to be honest with himself—he covered up some of his lust for power and greed for worldly things with philosophical and religious pieties. All in all, Augustine the sinner found it hard to make sense of his story. It did not appear to be a coherent narrative, and Augustine was not entirely sure who he was or where he was going. He was not even sure where he wanted to go (though he often pretended otherwise). This was a situation of severely diminished agency.

Augustine's agency was not so severely diminished, however, that he could not, at least to some degree, be blamed for the evil in his life, or praised for the good. Augustine thought that scripture made it obvious that God blames sinners, and rebukes and even punishes them. Doing so was practical not only for God but also for us because it may very well be the case that we, who care what others think about us, will be swayed by their rebukes or empowered by their admiration.[34] God often ordains our interactions with one another to be instruments by which we are offered teaching and correction.

It is fair and proper to offer such rebukes or praises because even fallen sinners have not completely lost the gifts God gave them when God made them—even persons who lack faith and proper love have the ability for it, and this elevates them to a place of distinction in the cosmos. Although the mere ability to be in a loving conversation with God is not enough to make us free, it is enough to make us responsible before God. Thus, Augustine blamed those who did not believe in God because it was their own wills that did not believe, and he gave credit to those who did believe because it was their own wills that did believe.[35] Likewise, he blamed himself for his idolatrous and self-seeking relationships, and his worship of goods other than God. He made it clear in his *Confessions* that in spite of the fractured nature of himself, it was nevertheless he who had willed career success, who had desired fame and enjoyed the admiration of his peers. He had been a fool, unwise and misguided. He could not simply say, therefore, that God had "made" him do these things. He had willed them; it was his voluntary agency that was in the wrong. In what might well have been a reference to his old self, Augustine noted that "...when someone says, 'I cannot do what is commanded because I am conquered by my concupiscence,' he, of course...recognizes his own evil in himself, and grieves."[36]

Of course, the fact that Augustine accepted his own responsibility did not mean that God did not share in that responsibility. After all, God was not only his conversation partner but also the one who made Augustine's testimony possible in the first place. God had permitted him to fall into these paths, and had not stopped him. But Augustine believed that God had done so for the sake of greater goods that God was gradually revealing to him, and which Augustine could begin to see as he looked back over his life. So while God bore some of the responsibility for Augustine's wayward life, on the whole Augustine sought to give God credit for the turns his story had taken. He did not think that he was in a position to complain. He did not understand all of God's ways, but that was precisely why Augustine thought it better to wait and see where God's story was going.[37]

A parallel point applies to Augustine's views about the agency of sinners who have received God's forgiveness and have begun to be transformed by God's prevenient grace. When God decides to turn a heart toward true love, as Jesus had dramatically done in the case of St. Paul, the target of God's love cannot reject the offer God makes. Yet Augustine sought to avoid fatalism by insisting that the grace God offers to the elect "does not destroy the human will, but changes it from an evil will to a good will and, once it is good, helps it."[38] Only via our own voluntary agency are we able to be genuine partners of God, which means that God's agency must work through ours if it is to be we who are saved. God may clarify our vision so that we are able to see what is truly worthy of love, and how to love well, but we are the ones who love. As our coauthor, the God who gave us our voices may enhance our voices, and influence what we say, but if we are to be genuine coauthors we must nevertheless speak for ourselves, from our hearts. God often speaks through us but God does not speak for us. So, Augustine urged, "Let no one, then, accuse God in his heart, but let each person blame himself when he sins. And when he does something as God wants, let him not take this away from his own will. For, when he does it willingly, he should call it a good act, and he should hope for [a] reward..."[39]

4. Predestination vs. paganism

Augustine's zeal for the doctrine of predestination may be the easiest to understand when we recognize the role it played in his own personal piety. We read in the *Confessions* that it was not until Augustine had begun to achieve all that he had dreamed of accomplishing that he became most confident that his life was being wasted. His (and his family's) plans had been fulfilled: he was engaged to marry up the social hierarchy, and had recently been appointed to a role as orator in Milan, the capital city, where he would have spoken before the leading generals, politicians, and churchmen of his day. These carefully executed plans were not, however, as wise or fulfilling as he had hoped; Augustine had begun to realize that the script he had chosen for his life was poorly written. At the same time, when he looked back on that time from a later vantage point, Augustine was amazed to see that his life, even then, had had a meaning other than the one he had thought of. Even in his mis-steps, God had been working in him. Augustine's *Confessions* suggests that he had begun to see himself as similar to the many biblical figures who had been called to serve God from their beginning, and who were prepared for that service long before they knew. He was predestined to be God's servant.

Such a perspective seems comprehensible to many of us even if it also seems odd. Yet the fact that we think we understand where he was coming from may cause us to lose sight of the ways in which Augustine was contributing to radical shifts that were transforming the ancient world into one more like our own. His doctrine of predestination played a significant role in that shift. The ancient world was familiar with the idea of fate, and in spite of his explicit rejection of fate in *City of God*, Augustine has often been accused of making that idea over for Christians. However, the two ideas differ in important ways. A world ruled by fate is a tragic existence indifferent to the plight of mortals, and only occasionally one where morality genuinely matters. The vaulting ambition of Ajax or Oedipus may eventually have been brought low in their tragedies but that same pride was also a key virtue of Achilles, essential to his greatness.

Augustine's vision of the world was radically different from his pagan forbearers, and much of the difference can be tied to his doctrine of predestination. Augustine's world is crafted by a personal God who started with a plan to create a loving community, who relates to each person as an individual, and who always gives no less than what is due, and often gives more. In that context, gratitude becomes a key emotion, and humility a key virtue. Augustine's God ordained varied intermediaries to mediate between ordinary believers and the sublime, but fundamentally the idea of predestination promotes a directness in the relationship between the human and the divine. It suggests that each soul is immediately related to its maker, who picks it to play some definite role in the greater story. In some way, then, even those who disobey serve their maker. This gives each person's story a value and import that it had lacked in Roman and Greek thought. Everyone's life is graced to at least some extent, on this account.

In addition, personal stories are given great depth, because they have meaning in them far deeper than any of the shallow stories we might recount on our own. To again take Augustine's own story as our example, consider his struggle, recounted in his *Confessions*, to make sense of his life. He spoke of a life in pieces, times that he had forgotten and events he could not make sense of. Some occurrences seemed important, but it was not clear how until later, or not even then. Some took on radically new meanings as time passed, for better or for worse. Behind all the shadows and mystery, Augustine discerned the hand of a master storyteller at work. He had come to think that living in faith required giving up on the idea that he had a particularly reliable or insightful understanding of the meaning of his own life. In part that was because he was still a sinner, blinded by his faulty notions and affections. More significantly, however, it was because of his creatureliness, which characterized him as a being whose story is composed in relationship with another. Only God could tell Augustine who he was, not simply because Augustine could not see himself clearly but because Augustine really was who his maker and savior said he was. The beauty of that was Augustine's realization that if it had been up to him to write his own life story, it would not have come out especially well. It was better, he thought, to be the subject of a brilliant dramatist who knew his character intimately. He was the better for it.

None of this is to say that there is no place in the Christian life for trying to make something of oneself, or for effort and striving. Rather, effort is put in its place by these comments. Augustine can hardly be said to have been without ambition, or to have been lazy. Few who have lived have been more hard working. Augustine's belief in God's direction of not only his story but all stories put his own efforts in their place, however. Augustine's work was communal, and his efforts were not his alone. The fact that they were secondary did not make them any the less expressions of his own drives and commitments. Augustine's psychological complexity meant that it still made sense for him to surround himself with friends who would challenge him to be his best, and practices of meditation, community, eating, and so on, that would bring the best out of him. Augustine's powerful suggestion that only the one who is the origin of our stories can finally make them make sense did not mean that he was not also an active agent who sought to make sense of his own life. It simply expressed his recognition of the limitations of his, and our, agency.

At the same time, the implication of the priority of God's gracious action in Augustine's thought is that those whose stories God only knows, but does not continue to coauthor, come to a bad end. This, plus the many evils that seem to exist in everyday life—as the book of Ecclesiastes says, sinners flourish and the good die young—raise the natural question of why, if the history of this world is a narrative that God is telling, the story of humanity takes the chilling and sad turns that it so often does. For all the brilliance of his discussion, this is a question that Augustine had difficulty answering. In the next two chapters, we will consider whether his greatest medieval admirers were able to do better.

2

Anselm's libertarian alternative

1. Anselm's challenge to Augustine

Although he lived in a different part of the world about six centuries after Augustine, Anselm of Canterbury was quite obviously influenced by his great predecessor. Many of Anselm's writings echoed the dialogical form of some of Augustine's best-known works, and Anselm at times imitated Augustine's openness in directly addressing God, praying for assistance as he pondered the meaning of his faith. These stylistic debts may have obscured from many readers the fact that Anselm departed from Augustine on important points of Christian doctrine, especially when it came to the topic of predestination and the issues connected most closely to it. In fact, the view Anselm developed would have been well suited to the concerns of the monks for whom Augustine wrote his books on freedom, rebuke, predestination, and perseverance. Where Augustine had stressed the lack of competition between divine and human agency, Anselm argued that it is important for there to be a space for independent human self-determination. God may give us the grace we need in order to become virtuous, but Anselm's position was that God does not push anyone into any particular moral or spiritual status—that is something we have to make of ourselves. This approach, Anselm hoped, would avoid the questions about divine responsibility for evil raised by Augustine's view.

In spite of their disagreements, Anselm sought to hold on to as many of Augustine's insights as he thought he could. Anselm's first

step in explaining his view of human agency was to appropriate
key ideas from Augustine. In *City of God* Augustine had made an
overarching contrast between two ways of living in this world.
There are some who love God, and go so far as to prize serving
God more than their own happiness, and there are the majority of
persons who prioritize love for themselves, and who are willing to
go so far as to make use of God for their own ends.[1] Anselm saw
that Augustine did not mean to condemn all love for self; Augustine
spoke too often of happiness as something we ought to seek. The
problem with the "earthly city" is not that it has self-love but that
its loves are out of order. It ought to love God above all, and other
things inasmuch as they conduce to and partake in love for God.
Finding this an insightful diagnosis of the human condition, Anselm
appropriated this idea for his own psychology, which he then used
to explain the fundamental movements in human history.

We can understand his view of all humanity by analyzing his discussion of how it was possible for human beings to fall. Augustine
had claimed that Adam and Eve were created with an overriding
love for God, and that the loss of that ordered love in the Fall was
psychologically inexplicable. God may have allowed it to happen
for God's own reasons, but Augustine did not think we can make
sense of why Adam and Eve found it attractive to pursue what God
had told them not to, rather than trusting in God to make things
right. Anselm, by contrast, sought to offer an explanation that
made at least partial sense of the Fall. God made Adam and Eve
perfect, Anselm suggested, but not stable. They were not able to
stay as they were—morally and spiritually speaking, they had either
to move forward or backward, and which direction they went was
up to them. From God's point of view, as it were, he suggested that
things were arranged in this manner because God had to give Adam
and Eve a particular kind of freedom of choice in order for them
to become genuinely morally responsible beings. From Adam and
Eve's point of view he offered a moral psychology to explain how it
was possible for them to fall.

When God made the first couple, Anselm proposed, they were
given two basic drives (often translated as "wills," or "dispositions").[2]
All persons have a will to seek their own advantage, that is, a drive
to pursue their own good. This desire is unavoidable, and appropri-
ately so, because God's creatures ought to value the life they have
been given and seek to promote it. Adam and Eve were also given a

drive toward justice. The challenge God set them was to relate these two inclinations rightly. To will justice is virtuous in itself, but to will one's own good does not necessarily lead to happiness. Given the way God made us, we can truly be happy only by primarily willing to be just, and secondarily willing to be happy. God's intention was that as Adam and Eve sought justice, they would each see to the other's needs, and thus both would be cared for, by caring for one another.

Thus, God made Adam and Eve with a drive for self-love and a drive for justice. Their desire for righteousness was not habitual or well developed, however, and could easily be lost. After all, it is reasonable to fear that willing justice may not conduce to one's own advantage. Such a thought could cross one's mind without sin, and was indeed brought to mind by the serpent's suggestion that service to God might require giving up on having a significant good for oneself. Having had such a thought, they were tempted to "play it safe" when they faced the hard choice of whether to trust in God's law, which they did not understand. And in the end, Anselm proposed, Adam and Eve did chose to prioritize their own happiness over upright dealing in service under God.

Having thus lost their uprightness by making this fundamental choice about their priorities, they found that they could not get it back. Anselm can seem at times to claim that the drive for justice is lost after the Fall, but that cannot be what he means. Even fallen human beings retain a drive for justice. Their problem is that the will to justice is always skewed by what has been established as a more basic drive to pursue our own happiness (or at least what might seem to lead to happiness; the irony of the Fall is that Adam and Eve are made unhappy by their attempt to prioritize their own good because they are so constituted that they could only have become truly happy by having entrusted their happiness to God). This is a problem passed on to Adam and Eve's children as well. Until and unless God hits the "reset" button, and once again makes this fundamental choice about priorities available to us, we are unable to reorient ourselves. Thus, all human beings need God's grace if we are to be able, once again, to fully and wholeheartedly will justice.

Augustine might have objected that Anselm's explanation of the human situation makes God out to have taken a huge risk, without a significant enough offsetting gain. After all, he had written to his Pelagian opponents that "innocence, if you pay close attention,

is a greater good than free choice."[3] Anselm, by contrast, argued
that God set this task before the first couple—and, by grace, sets it
before us as well—so that they could be good in a very particular
way. God wanted human beings to value goodness not simply
because it was necessary to do so, or because it was pragmatic to
do so, but for its own sake.[4] Anselm made a parallel point about the
importance of unconditioned free choice for the angels (though he
believed that unlike human beings they cannot be redeemed from
the choice that they made).[5] In both cases, Anselm's inspiration for
this idea may have been the way that God is the unconditioned
source of divine goodness. Nothing other than God's own nature
makes God to be good. To put the point differently, God is the sole
source of God's own goodness and there is no explanation for God's
goodness other than God. Anselm seems to have thought that God
desires to present us with the opportunity of similarly being unconditioned sources of our own goodness. Anselm also clearly believed
that only those who are able to choose right from wrong without
being conditioned to do so are deserving of praise, or blame, for
the state of their wills. Thus, he was what philosophers now call a
"libertarian" about responsibility, having believed that persons are
responsible for (and only for) what they choose without necessity.

Intriguingly, Anselm often sounds like he is not a libertarian
about freedom, or at least every type of freedom.[6] Not surprisingly,
this has confused some of his readers. Augustine had argued that
a choice about whether to sin was not available to God, who is
necessarily good, and that freedom therefore could not be defined
by having an ability to sin, as well as the ability not to sin. Anselm
follows Augustine on this point—freedom is essentially positive,
Anselm maintained, the ability to intentionally seek the good as
such: "...the liberty of will is the capacity for preserving rectitude
of the will for the sake of rectitude itself."[7]

Anselm also agreed with Augustine that God has the highest kind
of freedom—one that implies the impossibility of sinning. The first
couple had only the freedom not to sin, and their children lack even
that, though we all desire a freedom more like God's, whether we
know it or not.[8] Anselm and Augustine therefore shared the view
that God's freedom is the life of just goodness for which all rational
creatures were made, and it is the true goal of the agency of rational
creatures. This is the freedom that would have been bestowed on
Adam and Eve had they chosen rightly, and was bestowed on the

angels who did not fall. For Anselm, all human agency ought to aim at the freedom to live rightly in relationship that is intrinsic to who God is. He agreed with Augustine that any act that does not conduce to that end is not genuinely free. His disagreement with Augustine was not, therefore, about what it takes to have the highest possible freedom, but about the nature of human agency, and especially about the goodness of the kind of autonomous choice we have been discussing, which involves a lesser kind of freedom. The clearest way to put this point, I think, is to say that Anselm was a libertarian about responsibility who shared Augustine's conception of heavenly freedom as confirmation in the good. They both valued this normative freedom but disagreed about how earthly agents can achieve it.

Although Anselm did not discuss his disagreement with Augustine explicitly, he seems to have believed that God is a responsible agent, deserving of praise for God's perfections, because although God is a necessary being God is not under any necessities that are externally imposed. Although God cannot sin, God is not under a compulsion to be that way; God simply is that way. God, therefore, does not need choice in order to be free or to be responsible. Human beings, by contrast, are creatures, under many necessities that they did not constitute for themselves. If we are to become independent sources of the moral and spiritual qualities of our wills, God has to make special arrangements. The dual drives discussed above are one important ingredient that makes it possible to offer humanity a kind of autonomy. This autonomy is something we can only achieve by making a choice between good and evil that is not determined by anything other than our own activity in choosing it. Ironically, then, according to Anselm, the serpent was telling Adam and Eve a half-truth when it said that their choice to eat from the tree would make them like God. The falsity of its claim was that it was not eating from the tree that made them like God but rather the choice about whether to do so.

In order to make this choice possible, God also had to keep certain aspects of the divine plan a mystery.[9] For instance, if the first couple (or the angels) had known that choosing to prefer self over justice would not lead to happiness, they would have had no option but to choose justice—although they may have done so for its usefulness to themselves, rather than its goodness in itself. Ignorance was therefore another essential ingredient that made it possible for them to have an undetermined choice. This continues to be the case even after the Fall. For creatures, full knowledge of the meaning of one's choice would make choice impossible because it would be clear what to choose. To at least some degree, therefore, creaturely free choices have to be blind.

2. Anselm on predestination

Anselm's approach to creaturely agency made it impossible for him to share Augustine's perspective on predestination. If God's plan is for us to independently determine the direction of our own stories, God cannot also continue to coauthor our stories. Rather, God sets us up with the tools we need in order to write and then allows us to do so.

Describing Anselm's view thus might seem to lose sight of the fact that he too believed that human beings deeply need the ongoing grace of God. Yet as Anselm depicted it, prevenient grace does not turn us to God, as Augustine had contended. Rather, grace offers us further opportunities to make the right choice, and then strengthens us if we do make the right choice, in response to our prayers for assistance. Anselm believed that God wants to leave it to us to choose justice for its own sake, but he also recognized that sinners, lost in the unbalanced concern for self that they inherited from their ancestors, cannot regain an equalizing love for justice on their own. His solution to this problem was quite sophisticated. In order to restore to us the possibility of a genuine choice about who we will be, Anselm argued, God graciously restores the love for justice to a point that enables it once again to compete with self-love for supremacy. In turn, that makes something akin to the original choice possible. This, Anselm indicated, is an offer God makes to many persons—though, not, as he believed scripture indicated, to all. Only some of those persons take full advantage of God's offer, however, by affirming the priority of justice over self-benefit. Those who do are saved.

Clearly, then, Anselm did not share Augustine's doctrine of predestination (though he does seem to have shared Augustine's view that God does not offer equal grace to all). For Anselm, God does not elect persons for specific roles in the story of creation ahead of time. At crucial points in our lives, it is not God who directs our paths but we alone. According to Anselm's libertarian view of responsibility, our conversation with God must, at crucial points, be independent (not coauthored) if we are to be genuine conversation partners. In the strict sense, from an Augustinian point of view, this means that Anselm did not have a doctrine of predestination. Anselm laid claim to a different sort of doctrine of predestination, however, one that would also have an illustrious and influential history. Anselm understood the divine predestination he endorsed as the causal activity of God that is based on divine foreknowledge and is responsive to human choices.[10]

Like almost all ancient thinkers, Anselm took for granted that God, who is outside of time, and who created time, is able to see all events within time, including events that have not, from a human perspective, come to pass. God causes many of those events to come to pass, so in many cases God's knowledge of our futures is a knowledge of God's own activity. Human free choices, however, are determined by nothing other than the activity of each individual human will. This means that God is passive with regard to our choices. God responds to them, which means that at least in some small way God has given created personal agents the power to change God's knowledge and activity. Our choices are eternally and fully known by God, which makes it possible for God to take our choices into account from the beginning. Still, they are a key feature of creation that God does not control. Rather, we might say that God manages around human choices in order to direct the world to its proper end. Anselmian predestination is the divine causal activity that, from the beginning, responsively orders the world.

Although Anselm did not adhere to Augustine's doctrine of grace, it is important to note that he did not take a Pelagian view. To be sure, his fundamental instinct about the import of independent choice was shared with the Pelagians; both took for granted the non-Augustinian claim that we are not created responsible for our moral, spiritual, and other personal endowments, but we make ourselves responsible by a volitional act of undetermined choice. That choice, they believed, explains why certain persons are saved and others are not. God does not coauthor our stories but watches as we write our own narratives. For the Pelagians, however, God's only grace was the gift of our natural endowments, particularly our rational nature, which gives us the power to make of ourselves what we will. Anselm's conception of the relation between divine and human activity was considerably more complex.

As I have been implying, Anselm agreed with Augustine's doctrine of original sin, which states that all human beings born of man and woman are subject to a disordering of their loves, such that they prioritize benefits to self over a wider concern for justice. This is a state in which we are all stuck until and unless God grants us a special grace that operates on our hearts and restores the power of the drive for justice to its original strength. Anselm is Augustinian in his conviction that God does so preveniently, not because we did something to deserve this help but because God is gracious. God moves to us prior to our moving to God, and God makes our movement to the good possible. Technically, Anselm argued, we have a kind of free will—the ability to love the good for its own sake—all along. Yet practically speaking, we are slaves to sin without the help of God because we cannot make use of this power to choose unless our drive toward justice is strong enough, and not twisted by self-regard. Given these claims, Anselm can echo Augustine's claim that we have nothing that is not from God, even while not meaning quite the same thing by that claim.

Anselm thus cleverly sought to mediate between Augustine and his Pelagian opponents by giving God's grace priority while also accepting the claim that because God's authorship and ours are in competition, human responsibility requires a kind of divine absence. On Anselm's telling of the story of salvation, God's ongoing activity is necessary for human salvation, which cannot happen without a special grace. In addition, this grace is not something God owes to humanity; it is a gift. Unlike Augustine, Anselm was convinced that human beings can always reject God's grace. God's designs are not inevitably met, and God's agency can—as God intended—be trumped and thwarted by human agency. As a result, it is far more clear on Anselm's view that God is responsible for human damnation only as the executor of a decision that was not in God's hands. In this matter, God facilitates only what human beings have wished upon themselves; God becomes an actor in our scripts.

This attempted synthesis was shaky in a number of ways. The first is simply that Anselm's doctrine of predestination is hardly worthy of the name. Indeed, it seems more honest to say that Anselm gave up on the doctrine of predestination in order to make room for his libertarian account of responsibility. He effectively replaced

Augustine's doctrine of predestination with Augustine's doctrines of divine foreknowledge and providence. Far from seeing this as a criticism of Anselm, however, modern readers might consider this a point in his favor. Indeed, given the worries about divine responsibility for sin raised by Augustine's doctrine of predestination, it is natural to criticize Anselm not from Augustine's compatibilist point of view but for having failed to consistently develop the implications of his own libertarian principles.

For instance, we can ask how Anselm could consistently hold human beings who are born into a fallen condition responsible for their misguided priorities. Since they have not chosen their priorities but rather inherited them from their parents they are not responsible or blameworthy for them. Presumably, Anselm did not press this point because he agreed with Augustine's claims that original sin is worthy of blame and punishment, and that baptism is the only avenue of redemption from original sin. Since it is clear that not everyone is baptized (or martyred, which they considered the salvific equivalent of baptism), it would have seemed obvious to Anselm that not everyone is offered the divine grace necessary for salvation. However, Anselm's view threatens to become incoherent without a revision on this point.

The most natural way around the problem of how God could damn those who have been given no choice in the matter would have been for Anselm to have argued that God does give a potentially saving grace to all persons, even if they are not baptized. He might have been able to argue that the grace received through baptism is superior in some way—it is not clear that his theory demands that God give everyone an equal chance at salvation, so long as God gives everyone a genuine choice in the matter. Anselm, might, in this way, have continued to try to hold together a nuanced position that sought to make sense of scriptural indications that God elects some more than others. Or he could have made a conceptual move that would have put him closer to the camps of more modern movements such as the Baptists or the Anabaptists, and simply argued that everyone is given the choice of whether to love well or ill.

At any rate, it would be consistent for Anselm to have maintained that God offers all persons a grace that puts them in something akin to the original position of Adam and Eve, able to choose for themselves which love to make central to their lives. Given Anselm's conception of personal responsibility, it seems appropriate for only those who personally and intentionally make bad use of God's gift to be damned, since in that manner each individual would be cursed only by her or his own hand. Without such an emendation of Anselm's view, it is hard to see how God meets Anselm's own criterion of divinity—that than which none greater can be conceived.[11] For surely it is easier to admire a God who only punishes responsible agents who are blameworthy for their faults than a God who punishes some who are faulty but who are not blameworthy for it. If Anselm hoped to make an advance on Augustine's theology of human responsibility and divine election he nevertheless had to agree with him that God would not punish those who are not responsible for their sin. Adhering consistently to that principle would have driven Anselm further from Augustine on other points than he wanted to be, however.

3. Merits of Anselm's alternative

From Augustine's point of view, Anselm's adherence to the claim that we are only responsible for what we could choose without determination exacts a high price from his orthodoxy. The more consistent Anselmians are in developing their libertarian views, the more it becomes apparent that they must abandon a number of the theological convictions Augustine held dear. In particular, the Anselmian must dramatically reinterpret the doctrine of predestination as simply a teaching about divine foreknowledge. The doctrine of original sin would have to be reinterpreted as well, as the discussion above implied. That doctrine would become the belief that all human beings are born spiritually and psychologically unbalanced, unable to get outside of themselves enough to love justice fully and properly. That condition would not, however, be blameworthy, and would therefore not constitute sin from which humanity needs to be saved. Finally, we have seen that an Anselmian approach to divine grace must limit its power and efficacy, so that God's agency does not overrun created agents.

In our time, more than in earlier eras of Augustine's influence, this may not seem to be much to give up. We judge theological views (like philosophical and scientific views) not simply on their individual merits, but comparatively. Although some views are simply untenable, many are at least plausible and have their attractions; our task is not merely to ask whether an approach has problems but whether it is, on balance, more insightful and less problematic than its competitors. Thus, the fact that Augustine or Anselm's approaches to the doctrine of predestination are imperfect is not a reason to reject either of them. The task is to see which approach seems most inviting on the whole. In this context, it is relevant that in our day the influence of Baptist and Anabaptist "free-will" theologies has become so widespread as to have become commonplace. Even within more Augustinian traditions such as the Catholic, Lutheran, and Reformed, there have long been powerful voices of dissent, kin to the "semi-Pelagians" of Augustine's own time. What counts as Christian orthodoxy has, for most believers around the world, been reinterpreted along the lines that an Anselmian could embrace more readily than an Augustinian. What counts as a strength or weakness of the Anselmian view may, therefore, differ quite significantly depending on one's existing views about freedom and responsibility. Many readers will find Anselm's view attractive because they are already implicitly, if not explicitly, committed to something like his libertarianism about responsibility.

Augustinians should admit that Anselm's conception of free will was an insightful and creative attempt to mediate between Augustine and the Pelagians. He argued that God graciously offers us opportunities to make something of ourselves, for good or for ill. Such a choice was not for him the height of freedom but a necessary precondition of it, which makes it possible for us to seek the good for its own sake. Unlike many modern approaches, Anselm's libertarianism did not simply appeal to some sort of vague but innate power of will to make of ourselves what we please. One of his key insights was that significant human choices are motivated choices, and therefore choices that can at least to some degree be explained. Of course, like any libertarian Anselm too had to argue that what finally explains any morally significant choice is simply the choice itself, which is spontaneous. He could not offer any other explanation for why one choice was made rather than another. He nuanced this view, however, with the suggestion that partial explanations are both possible and illuminating. The psychology of human drives that Anselm offered made it easier to see why a person might choose either justice or self-love as an organizing principle; whatever choice is made becomes intelligible even if it is not entirely explained.

In addition, Anselm refined his libertarian zeal for human self-definition with the claim that humanity is unable to be whatever it makes of itself because it has been given limits, as well as a proper goal and direction. He emphasized that creatures with wills have natures and histories that matter. Thus, he did not suggest, implausibly, that we can be anything we choose to be. Rather, we are given a specific choice—one that flows out of the kind of creatures we are, made to love ourselves as well as others—that has quite definite consequences, given the sort of beings we are, the sort of world we are in, and the sort of relationships we have. Anselm's agents are free not because they are "free floating," never tied down to anything, but because they have significant choices that make a difference to who they become. They are responsible so long as their character and actions can be traced back to at least one significant and free choice, in which they autonomously set their own course in life. On the revised Anselmian view offered at the end of the previous section 2, all created persons have at least some morally very significant choices to make, but once they have made them they do not continue to have such choices because the choices that they make define them. To be a free agent is to be self-defined in this way, not to always have an open array of options. Thus, according to Anselm's view our choices matter because they set us upon particular paths. One of those paths will work out better for us, given who we are, than the other, but we cannot always tell which path we are on, or which path is the right one. And that seems true to our experience.

Like many (although not all) libertarians, Anselm explained the ability to be the ultimate arbiter of crucial aspects of one's own moral and spiritual personality by arguing that we have the power to change who we are as a result of our spiritual, social, and genetic inheritance by making deliberate choices about ourselves and our behavior. He adjusted this standard account because of his belief that we have this ability only by the grace of God's ongoing help. The power to will certain aspects of our own identities is not simply a power we have at our disposal. Anselm did not expect us to have complete control over our identities. He agreed with Augustine that we cannot be solitary sources of our own narratives; Anselm's hope was that we can be the arbiters of certain aspects of our narratives, writing key plot points that make the overall direction of our stories our own.

Therefore, Anselm thought of free agency as a capacity to define oneself in the context of a relationship with God and others, and he avoided a simplistic account of freedom as merely focused on choice. That is a strength, since the simple views he resisted are inhumane in pitting freedom against the ties that make human lives what they are. Anselm also neatly combined his sophisticated libertarian account of freedom with what had by his time become Augustine's traditional emphasis that the highest kind of freedom has normative features. To be fully free one cannot simply choose whatever one might want; one must choose rightly. Freedom is thus both a necessary feature of personal agency and, for creatures, a task that must be achieved. Given Anselm's conception of human nature, we can be free in the fullest sense only if we choose to prioritize the good of the whole. Heading in that direction turns out to fulfill us, and makes it possible for us to have all that we want. Thus, once again, an advantage of the Anselmian account is that it does not pit freedom against the relationality that is so crucial to human existence.

A further strength of Anselm's view is that it more clearly separated God's action from sinful human action than Augustine's approach had, yet without making God irrelevant to human history after Creation. On Anselm's scheme, actions that are morally and spiritually defining of a person's self are up to that person alone. The motivations God builds into creatures are relevant to their personal choices, but they are not determinative. It is solely human (or angelic) agents who decide which considerations will factor into their choices for good and evil. Likewise, God's providential and gracious action in our personal histories (as well as the history of the world more generally) makes a difference to the circumstances in which personal choices are made, but does not determine them. This gives God some sway yet it allows human beings to be ultimately responsible for themselves. Because we are ultimately responsible, whatever we make of our world and ourselves is charged to our account, not God's. This is a major attraction and motivating feature of Anselm's view—it distances God from sin. Permitting sin is part of the divine plan inasmuch as God has to permit sin in order to make it possible for personal creatures to become originators of their own moral personalities. But that anyone should sin, and therefore any actual sin, is no part of the plan. Augustine sought a similar outcome with his contention that sin is permitted but not caused by God, but the success of Anselm's move seems less contestable.

In light of these strengths, modern readers may find little to worry about in Anselm's view. To many, it will seem intuitively more appealing than Augustine's. My goal, however, is to offer a defense of the traditional Augustinian doctrine of predestination and the ideas that travel with it. The following two chapters pursue that task in a positive vein by attempting to illuminate why Augustinian doctrines of predestination might be more insightful and less problematic than is often thought. Later chapters will also take up Anselm's thought, critically and appreciatively, much as this chapter approached Augustine's. Some of my own criticisms of Anselm's view will be articulated along the way, although my final verdict on what approach to predestination might be most appealing will have to wait until the final chapter of this book. To bring the discussion in this chapter to a close, however, I consider one of the limitations of Anselm's sophisticated and appealing libertarian account of predestination and human agency.

4. The problem of foreknowledge

Anselm's doctrine of divine foreknowledge raises philosophical issues that are too complex to deal with fully here, and I will discuss it only briefly—but long enough, I hope, for the reader to see why the topic is a problem for Anselm and those who would follow his lead. According to the doctrine of divine foreknowledge, every choice human beings make, and every action that we take, is known to God in advance. Thus, it seems that whatever we do and are, we are and do necessarily. To be sure, this necessity is, as Anselm pointed out, contingent, not metaphysical. That is, if God knows that I will drink coffee tomorrow, I do not do so because it absolutely had to be that way (if God had not created coffee beans, I would not drink coffee, for instance). Rather, I drink the coffee given a variety of circumstances that are contingent. Still, it is necessary that I do so; God has known that I would from the foundation of the world. Even if God does not make me drink the coffee, I do not appear to have any alternative to doing so.

Anselm's response to these concerns was to insist that God's foreknowledge does not stop me from choosing among alternatives as I seek to make something of my life. This is possible because God (who is outside of time) merely sees that I choose the coffee from among the options I have. Since God is simply observing me make my choice, my choice is intact. Thus, according to Anselm, while it may seem that I necessarily make the selection God knows I make, there is and was in fact no necessity. My choice is the driving force behind God's knowledge, which would have been different had I willed it.

As Augustine argued, this is a tricky topic, and it is not hard to think of reasons to worry about Anselm's approach to the problems raised by the doctrine of divine foreknowledge. It is difficult to see how I can be in control of a choice that I have not yet made but which God already knows the outcome of. That choice is in my future, and it is already set, so it can be hard to shake the intuition that since God knows in advance what path I will take, I have no alternative to doing so, and thus lack a significant choice in the matter. There is a confusing recursivity to Anselm's view that might remind readers of science fiction of the problems commonly associated with time travel, where a person can paradoxically go back in time and stop him/herself from being born. In the case of divine foreknowledge, the paradox is caused by Anselm's claim that although God infallibly knows today that my future self will drink coffee rather than tea, my future self is under no necessity to do so. It is hard to see how he can back up this assertion. After all, if God knows that I will do something it seems as though I must. Again, the problem is not that I must do it because God's knowing that I will do it makes me do it. Anselm was right to point out that divine fore-knowledge need not be causal. Rather, the problem is simply that if God "sees" my future self drink coffee, then that is what I will do, and it is hard to understand how I could actually have any choice in the matter.

Combining libertarian free will with divine foreknowledge might make sense, but it might not. And it would seem best to avoid such puzzles and paradoxes as much as possible. Those who do not find Anselm's response to the problem of foreknow-ledge appealing can respond in various ways.[12] An increasingly popular approach is to double down on Anselm's libertarianism, as the "open theists" have done in recent years. On this view, it is better to give up on the idea that God knows the future than to risk undermining belief in undetermined human choices.[13] From an historical perspective, this is quite a concession—open theism abandons one of the essential elements of traditional Jewish, Christian, and Muslim doctrines of God in order to conform to a highly contested theory of agency. It does, however, provide a consistent libertarian position, one potentially more consistent than Anselm's.

A second potential response harkens back to Augustine. The Augustinian, as we have seen, argues that the problem of divine foreknowledge is no problem at all for those who accept a non-competitive account of divine and human interaction. From this point of view, God's foreknowledge may create some sort of necessity for human action, or it may not; neither possibility is problematic. What counts is whether God knows that I drank coffee for my own reasons, and in doing so expressed my personal point of view (that I like espresso, that I thought it would help me deal with a lack of sleep, or so on). While divine foreknowledge may very well make it less likely that I had an alternative (I could not have had tea, if God knows that I had coffee), this does not seem to imperil my ability to act in ways that bear personal meaning.

Surveying these options does not, of course, settle the dispute between Augustine and Anselm's approaches to the doctrine of predestination and the many complex issues that surround them. How they deal with the possibility of divine foreknowledge, and how they understand its significance should, however, factor into our assessment of that dispute. In the following chapter, we will see how Aquinas developed Augustine's views into a philosophical theology at least as sophisticated as Anselm's.

3

Destiny and freedom in Aquinas

In the popular imagination, belief in predestination is something for Protestant Christians, but not Catholic Christians (the fact that some Jews and most Muslims have believed in predestination is hardly noted). If Anselm was the primary theologian to whom Catholics looked to inspire their theology, handing over the doctrine of predestination to Protestants would make some sense. As we have seen, the way Anselm understood free will led him to a weak endorsement of predestination, at best. By contrast, the greatest teacher of the Catholic Church, Thomas Aquinas, offered a strong endorsement of predestination (strong enough that we will need to inquire in the following chapter how his view differs from John Calvin's doctrine of double predestination). Aquinas defended his position ably, with the help of a nuanced noncompetitive account of human freedom and responsible agency.

Aquinas's account makes such good use of Aristotelian philosophy that some of his readers have thought Aquinas was more influenced by his philosophical commitments than his theological commitments. In this chapter, I offer an Augustinian reading of Aquinas's action theory and soteriology as an alternative. My view is that while Aquinas unquestionably made extensive use of Aristotelian terms and ideas, he did so to elucidate Augustinian theological convictions. Of course, his Aristotelian philosophy impacted his theological views, and how he defended them, in a myriad of ways. The relationship between the two is analogous to the way in which a particular language impacts how its speakers think and express themselves. Augustine and Aquinas's views diverged in certain respects because their philosophical home languages differed. At the same time, Aquinas's intent as a theologian was to use philosophy to help him understand the logic of the Augustinian theological convictions he had inherited—including controversial Augustinian doctrines like the doctrine of predestination. Thus, although it is true that in Aquinas's thought, philosophy and theology are so deeply integrated that it is fruitless to ask which influenced him more, it is also striking that Aquinas typically used his un-Augustinian philosophical and rhetorical style to defend theological views deeply congruent with Augustine's.

1. Aquinas's Augustinian theology of grace

It is fitting, Aquinas argued, that God should predestine rational creatures such as human beings and angels.[1] It is fitting, first, because like Augustine Aquinas believed that creatures naturally desire ultimate happiness. Aquinas also shared Augustine's view that perfect happiness is only attained in God, by God's grace. Aquinas's claim that predestination fits a natural desire that created natures cannot by themselves fulfill suggests, intriguingly, that creation is in important ways oriented beyond itself. We might even say that for Aquinas (again, like Augustine) creation is, in significant respects, incomplete without grace. This need not make creation, on its own terms, bad. It is good, for what it is, but it is also a first step, teleological, on the way to something else. Correspondingly, created beings have a certain instability. Rational creatures, in particular, cannot remain where they are; morally and spiritually and physically they change and grow or become less. Without God's help they fade away—but they were made to want more.

Because we were made to want what God alone can give, it is appropriate for a loving God to grant eternal, abundant life by freely predestining. Aquinas made clear that this is not a gift that human beings can earn, or come to deserve. Those who are predestined should have merits and virtues, but they are not predestined because of those merits or virtues. Indeed, because God's election of some for the gift of eternal life happens prior to their existence, it is appropriate to say that the elect have their merits and virtues because they are predestined.

We can already see that Aquinas's doctrine of predestination shares a number of key features with that of Augustine's. Whereas for Anselm predestination is associated with divine foreknowledge of what moral agents will make of themselves, for Augustine and Aquinas predestination is a commitment God makes to place a plan for salvation in action in the course of history. Aquinas's formulation of this point is more technical than that of Augustine's. Aquinas wrote, "predestination is [an] ordering of some persons towards eternal salvation, existing in the divine mind."[2] In other words, predestination is a special part of divine providential care for creation, a destining that is enacted in history but imagined before the foundation of the world. According to Aquinas, if one wants to be precise, one should say that predestination is an atemporal decree, a command for life given by God prior to the start of time as we know it. Predestination also implies a providential order in history, however, because when God enacts that command in history we get salvation history, the activity of God's grace, which moves from creation through fall to redemption in the lives of individuals and communities, generation after generation. Whereas for Anselm predestination is a passive recognition, for Augustine and Aquinas it is active, powerful and effective, akin to God writing the plot of a story that God then goes on to make real. Creatures who come to share in the life of the Triune God do so because God has willed that they do so, and has graciously bestowed on them the means by which it is possible for them to do so.

In part because of the place predestination held within his doctrine of providence, Aquinas shared Augustine's view that predestination is always positive, a gracious and merciful act. Predestination, as they used the term, is always to blessedness, eternal joy with God. As a result, no one is predestined to hell, not even the devil. However, Aquinas did not believe in universal salvation. What then of those who fall and do not receive the gift of heaven? Such persons are not outside of the divine will and plan. Rather, for God's own good reasons God permits some rational beings to fall into sin and unhappiness, and to remain in such a state. Such beings may receive grace of various sorts, but they do not receive the grace of predestination.

Aquinas called this divine activity reprobation. Reprobation is something God does simply by not willing to save sinners, since it is only possible to receive eternal life through a special divine gift.[3] Although reprobation is intentional, a decree parallel to predestination, in that both are plans God makes prior to the physical existence of the persons being destined, Aquinas carefully clarified a key difference between the two decrees. Predestination has a kind of causality since God's will for eternal life is accomplished by giving many kinds of grace to those who are elect. By contrast, reprobation does not cause sin; it is the divine decision "to permit a person to fall into sin, and to impose the punishment of damnation on account of that sin."[4] Aquinas's Augustinian view was that nothing causes a person to fall into sin (and certainly not God, who cannot be the author of evil). God, however, can fail to save some from their sin, and this is what happens in reprobation. On Aquinas's view, God does will, in a general sense, that all be saved, but this general desire is more like a wish that can be thwarted than an actual decree, which in God's case cannot be thwarted. He put the point this way: "God wills all men to be saved by His antecedent will, which is to will not simply but relatively; and not by His consequent will, which is to will simply."[5] Thus, on Aquinas's view God does desire the salvation of all, but for various reasons what God has actually decreed is the salvation of some.

Aquinas also followed Augustine in seeing Christ's human nature as the primary example of predestination. Christ's divine nature is eternal and cannot be predestined but rather destines. Christ's human nature, however, is destined as an act of love not only for that specific nature but in order to heal and restore the human race generally. As the first (but not the last!) human nature to be given unity with the divine, Christ's human nature is the primary exemplar of not only predestination but also of all salvation, and it shows with particular clarity how predestination works. Christ's human nature was chosen before all time to be united with the divine Son, not because it deserved such an honor but as an unmerited blessing. How could it deserve anything, when it did not as yet even exist, and when it would exist only with such honor? Thus Aquinas wrote, "human nature in Him, without any antecedent merits, was united to the Son of God."[6]

As we have already begun to see, a second way in which the predestination of Christ is primary is in its power. Christ is not only the great exemplar of predestination, he is more than that, because

> Christ's predestination is the cause of ours: for God, by predestinating from eternity, so decreed our salvation, that it should be achieved through Jesus Christ. For eternal predestination covers not only that which is to be accomplished in time, but also the mode and order in which it is to be accomplished in time.[7]

The human nature of Christ was predestined in order that the other predestined creatures might receive eternal life through him. The elect are brought into union with God by the union between divine and human nature that first occurred in Christ.

2. Free will and voluntary agency

It is clear that Aquinas endorsed a doctrine of single predestination very similar to Augustine's. More controversial is the claim that Aquinas must also have shared Augustine's noncompetitive view of divine and human agency. Yet how else could he maintain that, far from being puppets of the divine will, the predestined have genuine agency and merits of their own for which they should be praised and rewarded, or that the reprobate have genuine sins of their own for which they should be punished? As we will see, Aquinas's defense of predestination was also deeply Augustinian, though it was developed in a more systematic and technical manner than Augustine's own view.

Central to Aquinas's account of free will is his sometimes overlooked statement that "punishment and blame is deserved for our acts because they are voluntary."[8] There are, of course, times when a person's actions are not voluntary, such as when a person is coerced by some force external to that person. Coercion thus excuses a person from praise or blame (or, at least, mitigates it, depending on the circumstances). For Aquinas, actions only deserve blame (or praise) when they are voluntary. But what, then, does it mean for an action to be voluntary?

Aquinas wrote that actions are voluntary when they are the product of an "internal principle" and are done for the sake of an end (or, we might more commonly say, a goal or purpose).[9] The way Aquinas spoke about the role played in human agency by intellect and will brought these two ideas together, since intellect and will are internal faculties that move us to act for a reason, and thus purposively.[10] Aquinas suggested that when we are moved to act by our intellects and wills we control our actions and therefore act with self-mastery.

Aquinas thought of will and intellect as separate powers, with separate job descriptions.[11] Although they are separate, they also necessarily work together, because each aspect of human psychology has something the other needs in order for it to do what it naturally seeks to do. In brief, the will is an appetite, a hunger for the good. As beings who will, humans naturally desire an end that is completely fulfilling—happiness. However, because the will seeks the good without knowing what is true it is, effectively, blind. In order to get the knowledge it needs to pursue the good, the will depends on the intellect (Aquinas, therefore, called the will the "rational appetite").

In turn, the intellect is able to make judgments about what is good. As beings with intellects humans naturally seek truth (though for a variety of reasons we do not always find truth, and when we do we often only find partial truths). As the faculty that seeks to make judgments about what is good, the intellect has the power to present the will with goods to desire, and to strategize ways to achieve those goods. This gives the intellect power over the will, but that power is not complete. The intellect does not simply lead the will around; they have a complex relationship.

By itself, the intellect is not able to motivate; for that it depends on the will. That relationship gives the will a certain kind of power over the intellect, since once it has developed some habits of inclination toward particular goods, it can encourage the intellect to focus attention on the things it cares for rather than other things. Think, for example, of the way our habits can be so deeply ingrained that we might eat certain foods without thinking when we are under stress. Because he thought that both the intellect and the will influence the other, Aquinas thought of the intellect and will as separate yet mutually interdependent powers of a created rational being.[12] They must work together if a person is to be an agent, yet they also sometimes work at cross purposes. When the will passionately desires something it can even overpower the intellect, at least to the degree that a person can do things that do not really make sense given the situation. One might, for instance, greedily eat too much cake even though what one really wants to do is lose weight.

Aquinas often distinguished the completely voluntary actions of rational creatures such as human beings or angels from the imperfectly voluntary actions of the irrational animals such as mammals or birds. The most significant difference between them is that although nonhuman animals have an appetitive power they lack the higher intellectual capacities human beings have.[13] Lesser creatures are aware of their objects of desire in that they see them as attractive. They want food or companionship, for instance, and work to attain it. Because of this they are able to act voluntarily, in a way. As a result we tend to blame or praise animals when their behaviors please or displease us, in a way that we do not respond to plants or rocks. Yet, Aquinas thought, such blame or praise must be qualified by the fact that the agency of "brute" animals is not fully free, because it is only partially, not fully, voluntary. Fully rational beings are able to act in a fully voluntary manner because they are able to rise above the mere instincts that drive animals. They can do so because they have awareness of the reasons they have to act, and the ability to consider whether the reasons they have are good enough to act on, or not. Human rational capacities give us a self-mastery, and therefore a freedom, that other animals lack.

We are now in a position to consider more carefully what, according to Aquinas, it means to have self-mastery. A major question he addressed in his writings on human freedom was the problem of whether freedom is compatible with necessity. This question was provoked, in part, by his view that we will the ultimate end of happiness by a "natural" necessity. As we have seen, Aquinas thought that no matter what else we want, we cannot avoid wanting happiness. That is simply how we were made. The will does not move itself from a neutral starting point, from wanting nothing to wanting something. Rather, it begins with a God-given directionality. It moves us to act because it is itself moved by the first mover to seek the good for which it was created.

Aquinas clarified, however, that although the will necessarily seeks happiness, this does not mean that in its particular, everyday movements it is simply moved by necessity. Aquinas's discussion of this claim was nuanced and complex, and has proven difficult to understand. Here is a representative quote: "in regard to some things the will is moved of necessity on the part of the object; but on the part of the exercise of the act the will is not moved of necessity."[14]

At one level, Aquinas's point is relatively clear. He was suggesting that perfect goods (such as God) necessarily attract the will, because they are exactly what the will was made to be moved by. But, Aquinas suggested, even such natural objects of affection do not force the will into action, because it is possible for the will to direct the intellect to attend to something else, effectively distracting itself from the goodness it would otherwise naturally seek. In turn, that is possible because no finite experience of goodness can fully mediate the good itself. Having said this, however, we may still be left wondering why Aquinas felt the need to make this point, and what its full implications are for his understanding of human agency.

Many of his readers have taken his discussion of necessity and the will to be presupposing that the robustly voluntary action he associated with free will requires the ability to do otherwise. As a result, they think he was arguing that a free will always retains at least a minimal ability to refrain from seeking even the most attractive objects. On this reading, Aquinas's point is that what makes the will free is that although it may at times find it cannot say "no" to something, even then it can at least fail to say "yes." If that was his point, he was siding with (and adding something important to) Anselm's libertarian view, which makes free will incompatible with necessity, and against Augustine's noncompetitive view, according to which free will is compatible with some kinds of necessity.[15]

There are two major reasons to doubt this reading of Aquinas. The first, conceptual, reason is that it makes Aquinas out to have offered a view of free will that is at best mysterious in its relationship to his views about divine predestination, and at worst inconsistent.[16] Aquinas's doctrine of predestination indicates that God can graciously transform the agency of sinners, infusing them with virtues of faith, hope, and love that count as their genuine merits. God does so by transforming the intellect and will, so that they seek the good and true, and are not seduced by the bad and false. It is difficult to see how Aquinas could defend such a doctrine of saving grace if he was a libertarian about freedom and responsibility. Indeed, it seems foolish to try to combine these two views. It makes more sense, however, to assume that Aquinas's position was consistent, and that his action theory fit his soteriology.

A second, textual, reason to doubt libertarian readings of Aquinas's action theory is that he made it clear in his discussion of choice and consent that he did not consider the ability to do otherwise essential to his account of free will. A helpful overview of Aquinas's view on this point is contained in his discussion of Christ's freedom and predestination, which as we have seen, Aquinas considered exemplary.

3. Christ's exemplary freedom

The proper act of free will [*voluntas*], according to Aquinas, is free choice [*liberum arbitrium*].[17] It might seem that one can have choice, and thus exercise free will, only if one's actions and attitudes are undetermined. However, in his answer to the question "Whether there was free will in Christ?" Aquinas clarified that his use of the term "choice" did not mean what *we* typically mean when we speak of free choice in a libertarian sense.[18] When Aquinas wrote about choosing he meant something quite particular, related to but different from what it meant to will something. In his lexicon, the act of willing means having an appetite for something for its own sake. In that sense, I *will* to be happy because happiness is worthy of desire for its own sake. More particular goals that I have are *chosen*, as the means by which I seek to achieve the ends I will for their own sake. Thus, I might perceive that being a friend is intrinsically good, will to be a friend, and choose to buy a present as an expression of my will. Often, such a choice is made among options. Happiness, and even more particular ends, like friendship, can be pursued in great many ways. However, there are times when reason may tell us that an end we will can only be pursued in one way. For instance, you might think that in order to be a good friend you really must do what you can to save your friend from an assault (assuming you are in a position to help). In such a case, your choice is simply to do what you deem obviously best; it is not a choice among options but rather a choice to act in the particular manner that properly fits your overall will to be a good friend.

Often, ordinary human beings have options to choose from because they do not know what is best. I might vaguely want some good end but have little idea of how to achieve it. According to Aquinas's view, however, Christ was far less ignorant than any other human. For instance, Aquinas believed that Christ knew what the point of his life was and how to go about fulfilling his goals. Christ's path to his crucifixion was not, for Aquinas, a case of choosing among a variety of options, including whether to obey the divine will or not. On the contrary, Jesus was too wise to see disobedience as an attractive option. Moreover, he knew exactly what the Father's will to save implied. On some views this increased wisdom and knowledge would actually reduce Christ's freedom, because it leaves him with fewer choices. However, it seems odd to suggest that the greater the powers of one's intellect the less free one is. For Aquinas, such views value the will in the wrong manner, by prioritizing its independence over its integration with the intellect. On his view, Christ's freedom was not an ability to obey or disobey, a dual ability for doing good or evil, but the ability to will the good, and to choose the means that accorded with that good. To live such a life involved choice, in Aquinas's technical sense, even if it lacked significant options. Indeed, Christ's life was more free than other human lives because rather than floundering about, attempting to discern what to live for and how, Jesus knew what was best, willed it, and choose appropriate means accordingly.

On Aquinas's account, Jesus was destined to take a definite path, the one that God had determined to be the way of salvation. As the second person of the Trinity, Jesus' divine nature had been party to that decision at the beginning of time. Jesus' human nature, however, had not. It only came into existence in the person of Jesus, already taken up into relationship with the divine nature. Aquinas seems to have taken for granted that its only option was to be conformed to the divine will. This might seem coercive, as if God was forcing something on Jesus' human nature, but for Aquinas it is simply a story of creation. There is nothing inappropriate about God's making Christ's human nature oriented to the good; that is what the creator has always done. Even rational creatures do not create themselves, but are free in being who they were made to be. And on Aquinas's account being created without sin did not remove the power of Christ's human nature to will or choose; it simply oriented his will toward genuine goods and choices. The freedom of sinners differs not by being greater but by being more incoherent, since sinners want happiness but then undermine their and others' happiness by making bad choices. Thus, when by grace their wills and choices someday become more like Christ's, they too will have fewer options but a greater freedom. Finally, they will be able to get the happiness they have wanted all along.

The fact that a lack of options is not a problem for Christ's freedom, but is in fact an asset, casts light on Aquinas's claim that "The will of Christ, though determined to good, is not determined to this or that good. Hence it pertains to Christ, even as to the blessed, to choose with a freewill confirmed in good."[19] As we have seen, it is sometimes thought that Aquinas was trying to rescue some sort of alternatives among which Christ (or, analogously, other free agents) could have chosen. According to this libertarian reading of Aquinas, although Christ's will must necessarily be good it derives at least a marginal freedom from the fact that it can choose among particular goods. One problem with this view is conceptual. Attributing Christ the ability to choose among broadly similar goods hardly seems to give Christ a significant capacity for self-mastery or self-definition. Even if he can do this good or that, he is still under a basic necessity to be virtuous, and his fundamental character is not up for him to choose.

It is doubtful, however, whether Aquinas was making the problematic claim some have attributed to him. The quotation just cited appears right after an argument that choice does not require alternatives or options because it can take the form of consent to reason's judgments in cases where there is only one reasonable way to pursue the good. It would be odd for Aquinas to have made that point only to then immediately take it back. Doing so would also have created an internal incoherence in Aquinas's view of Christ's praiseworthiness. After all, we have seen it is likely that given Jesus's wisdom and peculiar calling there were numerous occasions where he could not help but see just one appropriate path forward. It would significantly diminish Christ's freedom and merit if, on Aquinas's account, he was unfree in such situations.

A better way to understand Aquinas's concern about the determination of the will of Christ (and, by extension, other human wills as well) is to read him as making two points to clarify the role that intellect and will play in free agency. I use the term "free agency" here to escape our modern tendency to focus on the will as the locus of freedom. Aquinas made it clear that *persons* have free will because they are rational.[20] Thomistic freedom is a feature of the interaction between will and intellect, and thus of the whole being of a person, a free agent. Only together are the will and intellect free, and the better they are together, the more free they are.

Since, for Aquinas, free agents are rational agents, reason is central to his account. In passages such as those we have been considering, he reminded his readers that rational agency is not fixed on one thing because Aquinas wanted to safeguard the ability of the intellect to make judgments that arise not out of sheer necessity but out of the activity of reason itself. As he wrote at the beginning of his discussion of free will in the *Summa Theologica*, because persons act from free judgment, they "retain the power to be inclined to various things."[21] In other words, rational free agency requires a wide-ranging receptivity to reasons. That is what makes such agency different from acting from instinct, the way an animal does (or as we might worry, simply because of programming, like a robot).

Here we have a first crucial point about Christ's free agency. For Aquinas, "Actions are called voluntary from the fact that we consent to them."[22] Because he consented to the path God set, Jesus was a voluntary agent who deserved praise for his actions and attitudes. Consent, for Aquinas, requires sensitivity to reasons, but not alternative possibilities of willing or acting. That is why Aquinas resisted saying that Christ was *merely* determined to the good, one who acted as he did because he had to. Christ was indeed destined, and therefore it was necessary that he consent to certain goods. He was not, however, a puppet; he acted for his own reasons. His voluntary and rational consent was an essential part of the story about why and how he acted as he did. As a human person his causality was secondary to divine causality, but genuine and essential nevertheless.

This leads to a second point. Aquinas argued that the will has options about how it exercises its power in order to clarify the will's relation to the intellect. The will is under certain necessities, but these necessities are a feature of the interaction between will and intellect, not created in the will by the intellect alone. By itself, the intellect cannot make the will pursue any particular path. Even when presented with objects that are good in every respect, the will's wants can create distractions that draw attention away from those objects, so that they are not consented to. In making that point Aquinas was simply reiterating a core feature of his account of voluntary action already mentioned—the will is not simply dominated by the intellect but is, rather, part of a complex feed-back system. Aquinas was not being pedantic in making this point; he was trying to be psychologically realistic. Often we do not do what we have every reason to do, because we are not attending to our best reasons for acting. Instead of being focused on what really matters we might, for instance, be consumed with a video we happen to be watching or a stray desire that has suddenly taken hold. Presumably, the human nature of Christ is like ours, in that it too was able to act for less than its best reasons. These inde-terminacies do not mean, however, that Christ's will was finally undetermined, as if the will were a neutral power for deciding that is detached from reasons and desires but picks among them. Christ's will consented to what it found attractive, and what it found attractive is something that Aquinas ultimately explained by reference to God's action.

In summary, it is illuminating to consider the freedom of Christ's will, and especially the freedom of his human nature, because Jesus is thought to enjoy a freedom as great as human freedom can be, even though he often seems to lack choice as we typically use that term today. His human nature is confirmed in goodness by its relationship to the divine nature, and both natures are further constrained in their options by Christ's unique vocation. He was destined to save, and to do so in a particular manner. His freedom, then, is to will the path of salvation and to choose to implement the particular steps necessary to it, not some kind of mysterious potential to stray from his fundamental consent to the Father's plan. His unity with the Father is not only the paradigm case of predestination but the paradigm case of secondary human agency compatible with the necessities created by the divine will's activity in predestining.

A final clarification may be helpful. Readers of Aquinas have at times been misled about Aquinas's compatibilism, not only because of the passages already mentioned but also by the way Aquinas discusses whether the divine will imposes necessity on the things that it wills. He wrote that because

the divine will is perfectly efficacious, it follows not only that things are done, which God wills to be done, but also that they are done in the way that He wills. Now God wills some things to be done necessarily, some contingently, to the right ordering of things, for the building up of the universe. Therefore to some effects He has attached necessary causes, that cannot fail; but to others... contingent causes, from which arise contingent effects.[23]

Interpreting this statement is difficult, because Aquinas did not fully clarify what he meant by "necessary" and "contingent" in this passage. He can appear to take for granted that freedom is opposed to necessity.[24] This might make it seem that Aquinas rejected Augustine's noncompetitive account of the relationship between divine and human agency, on which my loving God freely is compatible with God's grace making it necessary that I love God.

However, Aquinas went on to explain that he agreed with Augustine's claim that those who are saved by God's will are necessarily so. He was able to do so by appropriating the distinction between kinds of necessity we saw Anselm use in Chapter 2. Aquinas pointed out that things can be necessary in either an absolute or a conditional sense (a claim that correlates with Anselm's suggestion that necessity can be either metaphysical or contingent).[25] What is absolutely necessary includes that which is conceptually required for a thing to be what it is. In this sense, God necessarily wills the good, and we necessarily will happiness. What is absolutely necessary could not have been another way. Conditional necessity is weaker. For instance, although Aquinas did not think God had to choose to create, once God does so Creation must exist. Conditional necessity is therefore contingent on a cause that need not have been.

For Aquinas, that which is absolutely necessary is not compatible with voluntary agency. What is conceptually required in order for me to be what I am is the basis for my agency, not something over which I can exercise mastery. At the same time, Aquinas agreed with Augustine that conditional (contingent) necessities, such as those created by God's grace, are compatible with voluntary agency. This is what he meant when he wrote that God wills some things to be done contingently. Aquinas was not going back on his claim that the divine will is efficacious, but explaining how. Christ's predestination created a contingent or conditional necessity that, on Aquinas's view, did not undermine voluntary agency, because the necessity he was under was produced by the loves and beliefs Christ himself had, given his nature.

4. Conclusion

At every point in his discussion of predestination, free will, and voluntary agency, Aquinas took himself to be building on Augustine's position. At times he sought to clarify or expand on Augustine's views, and this, combined with his dependence on Aristotelian terms and concepts Augustine did not know, sometimes led him in directions more or less subtly different from Augustine. Perhaps the main difference between the two great theologians is not what they taught about salvation but how they taught it. Rhetorically, the beauty and terror of the doctrine of predestination was foregrounded for Augustine in a way that it was not for Aquinas. Aquinas subscribed to these doctrines but he did not emphasize them, or engage in major disputes about them. Aquinas's theology contains much that is relevant to the pastoral attractions and dilemmas that arise when theologians teach about election and reprobation, but it does so in a cool and seemingly distant way. This sense of distance may explain why the doctrine of predestination is ascribed so much more to Augustine or Protestant theologians than to Aquinas. Aquinas's theology is misunderstood, however, when the central role played by the doctrine of predestination in his thought is not appreciated. Without this doctrine his understanding of the sacraments, his view of redemption, and his conception of the relationship between divine and human agency would be entirely different.

Like Augustine, Aquinas defended his doctrine of single predestination with a noncompetitive view of the relationship between human and divine agency. A central lesson taught by his doctrine of predestination is that God is ultimately in charge of the story of history. Because God is not only the first cause of all things but also the ongoing primary agent, God is able to create contingent necessities for voluntary agents that do not undermine their voluntary agency. By contrast, human beings ought to recognize that they have limited control. For Aquinas, self-mastery is not the ability to choose one's own destiny, or to make of oneself anything one might want. Rather, self-mastery requires having a right relationship between reason and will, or, put otherwise, between what a person desires and what that person takes to be true. True freedom is not merely doing what you want, but wanting what is good. Self-mastery, therefore, is a willing and perceptive submission to the sort of flourishing for which God made you. The relative weakness of this conception of self-mastery fits Aquinas's sense that human beings are fundamentally secondary in the order of things—yet nevertheless, as secondary agents, essential in the order of explanation.

To a significant degree, Aquinas shared Augustine's lack of concern about the theodical implications of the idea that God reprobates some, even if God perhaps somewhat arbitrarily leaves some sinners to reap the wages of sin. Yet Aquinas provided a clearer defense for God on this point than had Augustine. As we saw, Augustine found God's soteriological choices unassailable yet mysterious. Aquinas more clearly argued that God is in the right because God does not owe eternal life to anyone. Being created means receiving a gift, but giving that initial gift of life does not put God in the position of owing a creature eternal life. To be predestined is to receive an unmerited gift, one that is fitting for God to give but one that is not due. Thus, he believed, God cannot be criticized for failing to give it to anyone. One might worry, however, that this argument attends too little to the fact that not everything that is permissible for a person to do is particularly admirable. Even if God does not owe predestination to anyone that leaves open the possibility that setting up a world in which those who fail to receive grace necessarily enter hell creates significant tensions with a picture of God as loving and gracious.

4

Luther and Calvin's divine determinism

Aquinas, I have argued, sought to defend a doctrine of predestination quite similar to Augustine's, and did so in part by offering a theory of noncompetitive agency that, in spite of their significant philosophical differences, once again had much in common with Augustine's approach. Aquinas's return to Augustine signified a marked change from Anselm, whose Augustinian style of writing obscured, for at least some of his readers, the massive departures he made from Augustine's theology. The Protestant Reformers discussed in this chapter, Martin Luther and John Calvin, are like Anselm in that they both departed from Augustine's views in important ways. Yet they are also like Aquinas in that the departures they made were intended to assist them in faithfully representing an Augustinian point of view. Their departures from Augustine happened, perhaps not always intentionally, as they radicalized certain aspects of Augustine's views by emphasizing the points they took to be most central and stripping away the philosophical complexities that threatened to obscure those ideas. Even more than Aquinas, therefore, Luther and Calvin both retrieved Augustine and left him behind.

1. Luther's polemical context

In the rush to associate the doctrine of predestination with Calvin's theology, Luther's contributions to the doctrine and its centrality to his own thought have been neglected. Questions about predestination were central to Luther's famous personal crisis of faith when, as a young Augustinian monk, his troubled conscience led him to wonder whether God could possibly love a sinner such as himself. Reading a combination of Augustine and the biblical letter to the *Romans* convinced him that God did not base salvation on merit, but rather saves out of a love that does not depend on what sinners deserve. This, Luther concluded, was a far better way for the world to be, because "if it were not the purpose of God, and if our salvation rested upon our will and works, it would depend upon chance..."[1]

It is significant that Luther counterpoised divine agency not with human agency but with chance. To Luther's mind, the alternative to having God in charge of human history is not having human beings in charge, but having no one in charge at all. We should not think too highly of the choices we make, Luther suggested, for they are less self-determining than we think. We are subject to many forces, seen and unseen, and as a result we are not the powerful arbiters of our own identities that we proudly take ourselves to be. For that reason, Luther found the claim that God saves for the sake of grace alone not only more reassuring than its alternatives, but also more fair.

Luther's doubts about human agency are well known, as he intended them to be. Titling his major work on the topic *The Bondage of the Will* was not meant to be subtle. Rather, it was meant to remind his Christian readers of a central insight that, Luther believed, they were in danger of forgetting. Luther's career was motivated by a deep concern that the core Christian message— that God justifies us, and not we ourselves—had been corrupted. The gospel was under threat for two main reasons. First, Christian leaders had become selfish and corrupt. It would have been difficult for the Catholic Church to sell parishioners indulgences promising reduced time in purgatory for them or their loved ones if those parishioners knew that God's mercy is actually a free gift. Therefore, it was essential for the church to convince its members that salvation was at least partly, and in important ways, achieved by the works of human hands. This allowed the church hierarchy to profit off the hopes and fears of its members.

Second, and more importantly for our purposes here, Luther also worried that the Christian message had been distorted by centuries of Christian attempts to be philosophically subtle and sophisticated. Attempts to make theology more philosophical were not necessarily ill intentioned, but ran into trouble because of the difficulty of speculating about divine things. For instance, Luther railed against the following medieval scholastic slogan for being both essentially meaningless and extremely confusing: "everything happens by necessity of consequence but not by necessity of the consequent."[2] The point of the slogan, as Luther explained, was to clarify that what God wills to occur in creation is contingently necessary, since God might have chosen something else (an idea we have already seen Anselm and Aquinas discuss). According to this distinction, the election of the saints to eternal happiness is necessary, as a consequence of God having ordained it, but not in the absolute sense that God's own perfection is necessary. But, Luther wondered, what significant difference does that distinction between types of necessity make to our understanding of salvation? And how was anyone to know what the gospel really said when it was fenced about by such conceptual difficulty that even intellectuals had difficulty fully understanding it?

Luther's fear of philosophy coopting a proper gospel-oriented agenda expressed itself in a definite philosophical project, undermining Aristotle's influence on the theology of his time. Luther wrote that "He who wishes to philosophize by using Aristotle without danger to his soul must first become thoroughly foolish in Christ."[3] Accordingly, he had the courses on Aristotle in his university at Wittenberg replaced by courses on Augustine. This does not mean he was ignorant about scholastic philosophy, or Aristotle.[4] Unlike John Calvin, who lacked theological training early in his career, Luther was well acquainted with the theological schools of his day. Luther even lectured on Aristotle for a time, and one of his first works, now lost, was a commentary on Aristotle's *Physics*.

Luther was skeptical of the Ockhamist Christian philosophy pervasive in his day because he was convinced that it misunderstood human nature, and as a result approached morality and spirituality in a fundamentally backward manner.[5] Aristotle assumed that the point of the moral life is to strive to do the best one can with one's natural powers. Based on his knowledge of his influential near-contemporary Gabriel Biel, Luther took the Ockhamists' Christian appropriation of this pagan concept of the good life to center on the claim that God would reward those who did their best, and be gracious to them.[6] By contrast, Luther believed that reading Augustine and *Romans* had converted him from a fundamentally pagan morality, according to which human beings can and must be the authors of whatever meaning exists in their stories, to the true Christian ethos that God is the primary author of the goods in our lives. If the Aristotelian claim is, basically, that righteousness is achieved by doing good and that a proper education teaches what we should strive for, Luther offered the following as the true Christian alternative. Only those who are already righteous can genuinely do good; we cannot incrementally work our way up into virtue because our intent must be right in order to do good. A proper Christian moral education, therefore, teaches what someone else has done for me, which I might rejoice in.[7] Luther's ethos is apparent in his comment that good works "should be done as fruits of righteousness, not in order to bring righteousness into being. Having been made righteous, we must do them; but it is not...that when we are unrighteous we become righteous by doing them."[8]

A corollary of this view is that human worth is a gift, not a task. Luther believed that the error of thinking we can and must earn our worth had led the Catholic Church into a number of errors. One, as has been mentioned, was its teaching about indulgences, which suggested that it is possible to buy divine favor. Another was a kind of Pelagianism, the belief that human beings can earn God's love, and do so without relying on God's help.

It is widely believed that Luther's soteriological views were tied to a low estimate of human capacities after the fall into sin. On this reading, his claims about divine and human agency were motivated by the worry that sinners are too weak to make themselves righteous. This idea is misleading but not entirely wrong. Luther was not optimistic about the agential powers of sinners, and he considered the scholastic philosophical theology with which he was familiar mistakenly optimistic about the nature of human psychology, responsibility, and free will. However, the point Luther made in the quote above was mainly conceptual. Although reflection on the effects of the fall played a significant role in his thought, Luther's teaching had a wider theological base.

The core of his view was based on his conception of the shape of God's plan from the beginning—his doctrine of predestination. Even prior to the fall, the story of creation was not about striving to be worthy of God's love. If it had been, it would suggest, contrary to the doctrines of predestination and of divine immutability, that God's plan for creation changed after the fall. Rather, the plan always had been the same—for creatures to gratefully live out of the love God had already bestowed, celebrating a worth they could not earn but that they should embrace. For Adam and Eve, too, the goal was not to *make* their lives meaningful and worthwhile but to enjoy living out of the meaning and worth they were given to begin with. They too could will the good only by God's help.[9]

In order to make these points as clear and accessible as possible, Luther believed it was better to make succinct theological statements about predestination, salvation, and divine and human agency that stuck to the core of Christian truth. He did not want to be sidetracked by unnecessary philosophical complexity. Yet his attempts to clarify Christian essentials were at times so succinct and bare-boned that they have raised numerous interpretive questions in their own right. Two claims, in particular, stand in need of clarification. The first is Luther's summary response to the oversubtle philosophical distinctions mentioned above. "All things," Luther wrote, "happen by necessity."[10] Second, Luther wrote that "free choice avails for nothing but sinning."[11] Let us consider each of these claims in turn, and see what light can be shed on them.

2. Luther on foreknowledge and determinism

Luther's doctrine of predestination drew on the theologians— principally Augustine—who informed his reading of scriptural indications concerning divine election and human free will. As we have seen, Luther believed that salvation depends not on chance events, or human effort, but on God's eternal purpose.[12] Like Augustine, Luther found this doctrine appealing not merely because he believed that scripture taught it but because he believed that the logic of grace, and the necessity of Christ, pushed him toward it. Luther's doctrine of predestination expressed his trust that the arc of our life stories lie within the divine plan. Our lives are not merely events that God reacts to and attempts to make meaning out of after the fact. It is, Luther thought, reassuring that God does not leave questions of ultimate meaning up to us, but guides all things to a proper and fitting end. This led Luther to insist on the importance of the idea that the events of salvation history happen not contingently but by necessity. The Christian faith is, he stated, "completely destroyed" unless we believe that what God has promised will necessarily come to pass.[13]

Because Luther followed Augustine in tying his doctrine of pre-destination to his doctrine of salvation, it has been natural to read him as propounding a doctrine of single rather than double pre-destination. As we have seen, according to a doctrine of single pre-destination, God actively authors only stories of salvation. Like Aquinas, Luther spoke of those who are not elected by God as the reprobate. Where Luther differed from Aquinas was in the clarity of his insistence that both election and reprobation occur necessarily.

This theme in Luther's thought was partly an attempt to safe-guard the gratuity of divine grace. If salvation is something over which human beings entirely lack control, and is instead completely determined by God's decrees, there can be no question that it is by God's grace alone. However, Luther also based his claim that "all that we do, is done from necessity" on his belief in divine fore-knowledge and immutability.[14] "God foreknows nothing contin-gently, but...by his immutable, eternal, and infallible will. Here is a thunderbolt by which free choice is completely prostrated and shattered..."[15] God, Luther insisted, does not merely foresee what we will contingently do by our own choices, as libertarians such as Anselm and some of Luther's own opponents claimed. That would violate God's immutability, making God changeable, and indeed changed by human agency, because what God knew would depend on what we chose.

Luther carried this line of thought to the following conclu-sion: everything that happens occurs according to God's will, and is not merely permitted by it. "With God there is no contingency, but it is only in our eyes. For not even the leaf of a tree falls to the ground without the will of the Father."[16] Accordingly, he stated that because God foreknew that Judas would betray Jesus, it follows that Judas became a traitor necessarily.[17] Augustine and Aquinas would have agreed that what God foreknows happens necessarily, but in an effort to separate God from evil they suggested that some of what God foreknows is not willed by God, or only willed in a permissive manner. By contrast, Luther rejected Aquinas's distinction between God's antecedent desire for the salvation of the reprobate and God's consequent will to allow them not to be saved.[18]

Luther saw two problems with such attempts to weaken God's role in ordering the events of human history. First, he argued that such distinctions make no difference to our assessment of divine goodness. On Aquinas's view, God could elect everyone for salvation but for mysterious reasons does not. Since salvation is possible only by the grace of God, all who are not elect are necessarily reprobate, and God of course knows and wills this result. Thus, God just as surely condemns the nonelect on Aquinas's supposedly more forbearing picture of divine activity as on Luther's more direct account. Luther took his way of putting things to be more clear and honest. It had this virtue without adding any drawbacks to Christian thought, since he believed that his view does not create any more of a problem for understanding God's goodness than earlier Augustinian affirmations of single predestination had already created. Clearly, God elects to make evils of all sorts possible when God creates. That is the shadow side of the divine activity that no theist can pretend to fully understand or explain.

Second, Luther pointed out that the biblical story of the hardening of Pharaoh's heart, the Apostle Paul's interpretation of that story, and other biblical narratives (such as that of Judas or of Jacob and Esau) fit quite well with the view he was defending. On a simple reading, these stories present God as active, not passive, in the agency of those who oppose God's people. In fact, these stories explicitly indicate that the hardening of these antiheroes' hearts was planned so that God's glory might be displayed. Luther did not mean to imply, however, that God simply forced people to be evil, or to do bad things that were out of character for them. Rather, he suggested, God worked with (and not against) the evil that was already in their hearts, present through the power of original sin. Thus, God "hardened" Pharaoh by allowing "his own ungodly corruption...to advance along the path of scornful recklessness."[19] Notably, this sounds quite similar to the activity that earlier Augustinians had described as permitting. So what Luther really rejected was not traditional ideas about how divine and human agency interact—a point explored in detail below—but rather what he considered the misleading characterization of God's activity as passive or reactive. If God is acting in a way that makes it necessary for a person to be damned, through whatever means, Luther meant to call that spade a spade.

In making these arguments, Luther clearly moved away from what we would call a doctrine of single predestination and toward a doctrine of double predestination—but only via the implied claim that this, too, is a distinction without a difference. As far as he could tell, his doctrine of predestination was effectively the same as those we have seen defended by Augustine and Aquinas. On both views God selects who will and who will not be saved, and does not directly make anyone will evil but does intentionally and knowingly abandon the reprobate to their necessarily evil ways. The difference, to his mind, was that he was more straightforward about the implications of the doctrine of predestination than most theologians are willing to be.

From our perspective, the most significant difference between Luther's doctrine of predestination and that of Augustine and Aquinas is Luther's clear affirmation of a doctrine of divine determinism. If sinners are divinely determined that would seem to put God in a somewhat different relation to their evil than God has on Augustine or Aquinas's views. Luther did not, however, put much effort into developing the implications of his determinism, except on a few points where it was central to his soteriology. Whether in his *Lectures on Romans* or the long excursus on predestination in his *Genesis Commentary*, Luther evinced little interest in adjudicating complex or precise details of his ideas about foreknowledge or predestination.[20] He was more concerned about the pastoral and, one might say, psychological effects of the idea of election.

In his view, it is unprofitable for theologians to try to search into the hidden mysteries of God, and to speculate about what they might mean or how they might make sense. We are not in a position to understand the depths of the divine nature or plan, or the full meaning of the events that happen around us. It is more uplifting, and more pastorally appropriate, to avoid speculation and focus instead on God's revealed will, and the mercy of God that is taught therein. It is a particular mistake, he emphasized, to seek some surety of the end of one's story by searching for clues midstream. Because salvation is an unmerited gift, and the gracious God who redeems remains full of surprises, we cannot infer whether we are saved or damned via self-examination. At the same time, Luther did not recommend a pious agnosticism about whether one was a member of the elect. Those who hear the preaching of the Word should live a life of hope that finds repeated reassurance in the gospel promises and in the sacraments. To have faith is to allow one's own understanding of the apparent meaning of one's life to be recontextualized by the greater things God is accomplishing, and to trust that the meaning of one's life may, in Christ, be far more joyous than it might presently seem.

3. Lutheran freedom beyond choosing

Try as Luther might to avoid speculation, philosophical or otherwise, his doctrine of predestination inevitably raised deep questions about how God can blame sinners who are acting under God's own determinations. Luther engaged such questions not merely to defend his soteriology but to expand on it. His pastoral concerns about how the doctrine of predestination should be put to use within the church (for hope, not despair) found a parallel in his interest in dealing with the questions of fairness that the idea of predestination naturally raises. As a result, he wrote a book to take up these and related problems, *The Bondage of the Will*.

Many of Luther's readers have found this treatise difficult to comprehend, and troubling. The view he defended has widely been accused of promoting the depressing and fatalistic idea that human agency does not count for anything significant. Many Luther scholars have, therefore, attempted to marginalize *Bondage of the Will*, claiming that Luther's claims in the text were defensive, hasty, or imprecise.[21] It is, however, the only work in which Luther attempted to lay out his view of human agency in a thorough manner. Moreover, Luther explicitly stated later in his life that he considered it one of his best and most important works. In response to a proposal to collect his writings he wrote "I am quite cool and not at all eager about it because, roused by a Saturnian hunger, I would rather see them all devoured. For I acknowledge none of them to be really a book of mine, except perhaps the one On the Bound Will..."[22]

One of the reasons why Luther's readers have had trouble with this book is because they have not always had the philosophical knowledge to see what Luther was arguing. Here I offer a reading of what Luther was up to in *Bondage of the Will* that assumes he was building on some of the ideas Augustine developed in his late anti-Pelagian writings. That assumption is warranted, in part, by the fact that Luther clearly drew heavily from those Augustinian treatises in writing his own book. Luther even took the title for his book from Augustine's talk of an "enslaved volition" in *Against Julian*. My contention is that attending to the Augustinian background of Luther's argument that "free choice without the grace of God is not free at all" makes it possible to appreciate Luther's best insights and avoid common misreadings of his argument.

Luther's view of human agency in *The Bondage of the Will* is hard to understand, in part, because it is expressed polemically and somewhat unsystematically. Rather than being a positive statement it is defensive, an attack on Erasmus of Rotterdam, in response to whom the book was written. The deeper problem, however, lies in the fact that Luther's treatment of human agency dispensed with some of the rich moral psychology and philosophical terminology that Augustine developed in his polemics against the Pelagians. This was not merely an accidental feature of Luther's treatise. As we have seen, he sought to avoid dabbling in philosophy, deciding it better to avoid human speculation and hew more closely to the central gospel insights he sought to defend. Yet Luther could hardly avoid having his own relatively rich Augustinian moral psychology, which was both explicitly and implicitly developed in his claims about divine and human agency.

When Luther wrote that the sinner is unable to earn God's favor through his works, he had in mind not only the basic theological claim that human beings are ungrateful if they seek to earn the favor God freely bestows, but also a claim about human psychology. Although Luther's moral psychology was less complex than Augustine's, the outlines of his view were distinctly Augustinian. Luther's terminology differed from that of Augustine's, and his way of putting things was typically more radical, but like Augustine he sought to defend the view that divine and human agency are non-competitive. Luther did so by espousing a version of Augustine's compatibilism, which thinks of human agency as compatible with volitional and theological necessities.

When Luther infamously wrote that "free choice avails only for sinning," it is fruitful to interpret him as having had a number of Augustinian points in mind. The most obvious of these points is Augustine's claim that our choices (*arbitrium*) flow from the more basic orientation provided by our deep-set beliefs and desires (*voluntas*).[23] Luther made this point most clearly in his writing about sinners, with his insistence that our choices are not free so long as they are tied to fundamentally sinful hearts and minds. Yet although *Bondage* focused on sinners, this should not distract us from noticing the moral psychology that Luther believed all human agents share. Luther believed that both sinners and saints "do what is in them," in the sense that they can choose only what they are motivated to choose.[24] The most fundamental human motivations are aspects of personality that are too deeply imbedded within human hearts and minds to be objects of choice. Saints and sinners make their choices because of who they are; they are not, Luther thought, able to choose who they are.

Luther developed this claim with two striking metaphors. The most famous was his image of the human will as a beast of burden, subject to one of two riders, either God or Satan. To be subject to God is "royal freedom" but to be subject to Satan is mere bondage.[25] Similarly, Luther often referred to human beings as trees, bearing whatever fruit naturally results from a person's roots. Human beings make their choices because of who they are; as dependent beings they are not able to choose their most basic personal characteristics. These metaphors were his own, but in using them Luther sought to distill the implications of Augustine's anti-Pelagian writings.

It follows from Luther's claim that human beings do what is in them that persons infected with original sin lack "the capacity to do anything but sin."[26] Luther's readers have tended to focus on the idea that sinners lack alternatives, but for Luther the sinners' fundamental problem is not simply a lack of options, but a lack of significant choices. Sinners can choose all sorts of things, but they are unable to choose what matters most—to love well and believe rightly. The sin from which all sinful choices stem is lack of faith in God, in whose love the sinner is not content to rest.[27] Original sinners' problem is that all of their choices flow from this basic and flawed source, the unwillingness to let God be God. As a result, they are condemned to foolish attempts to be creators of value in God's place. In summary, then, sinners are like saints in that they both have volitional necessities—things they will inevitably choose given their core beliefs and desires. The difference, as Luther's metaphor of the will as a beast of burden suggests, is not that the saints have more choices but that their necessities are more blessed. Saints are necessarily oriented outside themselves, toward the true and the good, whereas sinners are necessarily curved in on themselves.

Confusingly, although Luther thought it best to give up on the ideas of free will or free choice in sinners, he granted that "you might perhaps rightly attribute some measure of choice to man, but to attribute free choice in relation to divine things is too much."[28] He developed this claim with the suggestion that human beings may have some options regarding "what is beneath them," such as what we have for breakfast today or how we use some of our possessions.[29] His idea seems to have been that although he himself was committed to divine determinism, it would be possible to grant, without giving away anything of real theological importance, that human beings may have something like the freedom libertarians seek in relation to spiritually insignificant matters. Luther did not speculate about how that might be possible, given his otherwise consistent acceptance of divine determinism; he simply stipulated that it occurs in ways that do not violate his commitment to divine foreknowledge and the priority of grace. In accordance with those commitments, he sought to clarify that his claims about determinism could perhaps be tempered in various ways, just as long as they did not undermine the central affirmation that God is the decisive figure with regard to "what is above [us]," matters that pertain to salvation.[30]

An implication of the interpretation I have been offering so far is that we need not read Luther as having taken the position that sinful human beings lack the power to make alternative choices of any sort. More essential to his view than a strict and thoroughgoing determinism was a claim about the significance of human choices and the control those choices give human agents. For Luther, whatever alternatives fallen human beings may choose among are, without the help of God's grace, morally and spiritually insignificant. For example, eating this or that piece of bread for breakfast might be up to you, but it hardly matters in the larger scheme of things.

This claim—that sinful human beings lack significant free choices, and do not therefore control the deep content of their hearts or the ultimate meanings of their lives—should not be equated with the fatalistic claim that human agency does not matter, or counts for nothing. Luther believed that what a person wills does matter. Indeed, he did not think a person could be properly understood without reference to that person's volitional and epistemic powers. What each person loves and puts her or his faith in makes all the difference to who that person is. Luther's polemic against choice was, therefore, meant not as an embrace of fatalism but as a rejection of the libertarian claim that there is "a power of the human will by which a man can apply himself to the things that lead to eternal salvation, or turn away from them."[31] His point was that the sort of choice sought by leading thinkers of his time, including his onetime ally in reforming the church, Erasmus, is nonexistent. Human beings have no such thing as significant libertarian free choice, because every important thing we do is done by necessity, in accordance with God's plan. Here Luther made an important advance on Augustine's theory of agency, by focusing more explicitly on the question of whether we have significant choices, rather than simply on whether we have some choices at all.

It is natural to wonder why Luther thought that sinners and saints can be blamed or praised for their actions if they lack significant choice about who they are and what they do. In his response to this question, Luther sought to clarify that even sinners, who are in bondage, are not compelled or coerced to be who they are or do what they do: "when human beings are without the Spirit of God they do not do evil against their will, as if they were taken by the scruff of the neck and forced to it...but they do it of their own accord and with a ready will."[32] Wills that are in bondage to evil are not free, in the elevated, virtue-oriented sense in which Luther and Augustine used that term—a point I will return to below. At the same time, Luther agreed with Augustine's claim that sinners are responsible agents who act willingly. As a theologian who accepted a noncompetitive view of the relationship between human and divine agency, Luther's answer to the question of what makes postlaparian sinners responsible before God for the unbelief they cannot help having was (in part) that they are not forced into that unbelief but rather believe as they do for their own reasons and in consonance with their own wills. In accordance with that view, Luther argued that divine judgment on sinners is a clue that points to the significant sort of agency human beings have.

Like Aquinas, Luther took for granted that only human beings and angels can be blamed as sinners because only they have the volitional and rational powers that allow persons to be either the image or the anti-image of God. Human beings, fallen or unfallen, are differentiated from mere animals by the fact that they possess an aptitude for a personal relationship with God.[33] This aptitude is the ability to partner with God willingly, in the manner only a rational creature can. Luther highlighted the fact that Judas and other biblical sinners were not under compulsion when they sinned. God neither forces them to sin against their wills, he insisted, nor takes away their agency; they acted willingly. So while sinners cannot do what they ought to, that is because they do not want to. Their bondage is imposed by their own volitional make up. Sinners cannot believe that their worth and standing come from outside themselves, and as a result they continually seek to justify their own existence. That is why they cannot turn from sin. Such a state of personal evil desire was, for Luther, blameworthy in itself.

I have been offering a reading of Luther as an Augustinian compatibilist. Although Luther's language differed from Augustine's in any number of ways, for polemical and cultural reasons, he made many similar conceptual moves. Like Augustine and Aquinas, Luther concluded that Christian teaching about sin and grace shows that although human responsibility is not compatible with compulsion, it can be compatible with divine determination. Applying to Luther a modern term for thinkers who consider responsibility compatible with necessity ("compatibilist") is, of course, anachronistic. Yet Luther's view fits neatly into the category, and it is better to call him something he would not have called himself than to mistake him for a fatalist. When he attacked the idea of free choice, he was not attacking the claim that human agency matters, but arguing about how our agency matters. He believed that even persons in bondage to sin can be accountable agents, and he rejected not the idea of human freedom in itself but the libertarian notion that freedom means being "master of my fate, captain of my soul."

A key to properly assessing Luther's view of human agency is recognizing the fact that he followed Augustine (and to an extent, Aquinas) in reserving the term "freedom" for those who are good. On their "normative" view of freedom, only God and human beings and angels who live within God's grace are free. In keeping with the moral psychology just sketched, Luther's normative conception of freedom did not require a libertarian power to choose among contrary options. The idea that freedom is asymmetrical (tied to the good) is strongly implied by the Lutheran metaphor we have discussed of the human will as a beast of burden, subject to God or Satan. There is a kind of necessity, Luther acknowledged, in the activity of those who are genuinely oriented to the good; like God, they are unable to do badly. Augustine had called this a "blessed necessity," and Luther followed him by emphasizing that such a necessity is internal to the psychical structure of the good person.[34] Luther sometimes called this the "necessity of immutability." His terminology sounds strange to us but we have a similar concept. What we would call a "volitional necessity," such as parental love for a child, is not experienced as compulsion or coercion, but as a natural outgrowth of who a person is. Such love can be both unavoidable and free.

Luther's belief that agency under grace is free—and that only agency under grace is free—makes a significant claim about human ontology. One crucial aspect of salvation is God's gracious remaking of the sinner's heart, to desire what is genuinely good for her or him. Luther famously described the sinner as *"incurvatus in se,"* turned in on oneself. The need to validate oneself focuses one's gaze upon oneself. Those who are genuinely good, by contrast, look outward without fretting about themselves. Divine grace frees them to attend to others. That grace cannot be resisted, but since a person's fundamental orientation is itself what grace repairs, those who are given grace do not resist, and are not compelled. It was important for Luther that Christians say "I am yours" to the Spirit, even though they cannot say "I am not yours." God recreates Christians not to overwhelm their agency but so that they might follow the original plan of creation and cooperate with him. Thus, Luther insisted that "[God] does not work within us without us."[35]

While there is a sense in which the Christian is "slave and captive" to the Spirit, in Luther's view human beings are always worshipping some god or other. Bowing to our creator and redeemer, who gives persons their worth and asks them to rest in it, is the only way to have the royal freedom that makes it possible to be so free from existential need that they can follow Christ in being lords of all and yet at the same time be the servants of all.[36] This elevated servitude counted paradoxically as freedom for Luther because he agreed with Augustine, Anselm, and Aquinas that true liberty lies in the direction God made us for. Luther's innovation was that he radicalized Augustine by speaking of freedom in no other way.

For Luther, those who are genuinely free are perceivers of truth and lovers in right relationship. Luther's Christian conception of freedom was characterized not only by the ability to live out one's loves but also by the life in love that is divine. Those who act willingly are responsible for who they are, but only human beings who are "little Christs" are free.

To sum up, although Luther's doctrine of predestination and his unwillingness to speak of sinners as free has led to criticism that he did not take human agency seriously, Luther actually propounded a fairly rich view of human agency (albeit one that can be difficult to tease out without a good deal of work). He followed Augustine in reserving the term "freedom" for those creatures who the Apostle Paul said are "free indeed"—the human beings and angels who respect the Sabbath nature of our existence by resting in God's grace. Luther presumed that freedom implied responsibility, but as we have seen, he did not consider the "royal" freedom of which he spoke to be a requirement for responsible and accountable agency. That might strike us as odd, since we are used to associating or even conflating the ideas of free will and of responsibility. But that by itself is not a good reason to reject his view.

Luther could have made his claims more clear—and his picture of human agency less minimal—had he developed a more complex philosophy of action. However, for pastoral reasons he decided to abandon the notions of "free will" or "free choice" rather than attempt to re-describe them in a way that challenged the Ockhamist libertarianism dominant in his day. Rather than defining free choice as the ability to do what you will (as Calvin later did), Luther simply argued that there is no such thing as free choice. He found more sophisticated views misleading. It is better, he thought, for us not to think that our powers are more significant than they are. In his experience, that way led to despair. The pastor's task is to remind the faithful to rely fully on God, in whom their hope rests.

Despite their philosophical limitations, Luther's views, read against the backdrop of the Augustinian tradition he sought to revive, were sophisticated enough to offer an indication of why predestination need not undermine human responsibility or accountability. Luther argued that grace does not undermine human responsibility because the transformation of the heart does not compel a person against her or his will, but rather reorients that person's will. The recipient of such grace might very well be said to be a new person—but that need not undermine the agency of the new creation who gratefully says "I am yours" to God and neighbor. Moreover, because that grace orients a person to the good that God always meant for her or him, it is conducive to human freedom. Thus, predestination to friendship with God need not be unfair. It may be more than fair, since God is merciful in not having simply left sinful humanity to its own devices.

It might nevertheless seem questionable for God to create beings God foreknows will be stuck in sin if God does not intend to help them. This, plus the many evils that exist in everyday life continued to raise the difficult question Augustine had faced— why the story of humanity takes the chilling and sad turns that it so often does. Luther's action theory allowed him to argue that those who are in bondage to sin are culpable because they sin willingly. They say "I am not yours" to God, who takes them at their word. Still, even those who accept Luther's view might be inclined to blame God for making those persons or for failing to assist them, unless God has good reasons for doing so. At this point, the question shifts away from questions of human agency to what we now call the problem of evil.[37] On these questions, as we have seen, Luther typically maintained a studied silence. These are questions Luther found difficult to answer, and rather than engage in speculation that might trivialize the problem he spoke mysteriously of God's hiddenness. He did, however, also echo Aquinas's claim that it is a mistake to believe God owes creatures anything. Moreover, as a divine command theorist he considered it conceptually impossible for God to be in the wrong.[38] If God desires to punish as well as heal, who are we to grumble? As Calvin memorably put it, "Monstrous indeed is the madness of men, who desire to subject the immeasurable to the puny measure of their own reason."[39]

4. Calvin's appropriation of Luther

Calvin is widely given blame and credit for being *the* Christian advocate of predestination not because he was the first to propound the view, or because his views were particularly original, but because he accessibly summed up traditional teaching of the doctrine and fearlessly spelled out its implications. The discussion of predestination in his *Institutes of the Christian Religion*, which he intended for a wide audience, has found an even wider and more durable audience than he likely imagined. But Calvin's pedagogical usefulness has led to any number of misleading claims about his views.

Calvin is known to many as the definitive advocate of a doctrine of double predestination, although that term was not known to him. By itself, the fact that the term "double predestination" is anachronistic does not mean that we should never describe Calvin's view using that term. We should, however, be careful to specify the meaning of that term so that we do not use it to tar Calvin unfairly. Calvin's theology of predestination and his correlated views of human and divine agency have been widely misunderstood, perhaps mainly for the following two reasons. First, Calvin's teaching on predestination is rarely read in its historical context. Thus, he has been made out to be a thought leader on points where he was a follower of Luther, as well as Augustine (who he cites incessantly) and Aquinas (who he seems to have known well enough to dispute on some minor points of disagreement). Ironically, he has also been mistaken for a follower on some topics where he actually sought to correct Luther by retrieving more of Aquinas and Augustine's philosophical views. Second, Calvin's interpreters typically focus on his well-known *Institutes* while ignoring important shorter works including his *Concerning the Eternal Predestination of God* and *The Bondage and Liberation of the Will*. Both books were written after his early drafts of the *Institutes* but influenced the final version of that treatise, which means that they both develop and clarify the views of agency and predestination Calvin developed in his *Institutes*.

Luther had highlighted the centrality of predestination to his conception of salvation, and Calvin followed him in this, placing his doctrine of predestination in the *Institutes* after his discussion of soteriology. In doing so, he separated his doctrine of predestination (which is placed fairly late in the *Institutes*, as a capstone of his doctrine of salvation) from his doctrine of providence (which is placed fairly early in the *Institutes*, as part of his doctrine of God). Some have suggested that in making this move Calvin was rejecting the traditional Augustinian conception of predestination as a part of the doctrine of providence. However, this wildly overstates the significance of Calvin's decision about how to organize his material. It is true that Aquinas's discussion of predestination focused mainly on expounding the divine causality in a theoretical manner, whereas Calvin and Luther emphasized the pastoral, experiential elements of the good news of God's sure salvation. These differences in emphasis lead to very real differences in the way their doctrines of predestination feel to their readers. All of these theologians, however, understood predestination in remarkably similar ways. As Calvin put it, predestination is "God's eternal decree, by which he compacted with himself what he willed to become of each man."[40] For Calvin, like Augustine and Aquinas, predestination is not a kind of foreknowledge, but a plan to enact an outcome that determines the ultimate destiny of each human being, and thus a central part of divine providence.

Calvin did not, however, follow Augustine in inferring that predestination is therefore always to be thought of as a kind of grace. Instead of distinguishing predestination and reprobation as two separate orders, one of grace and one of privation, Calvin described predestination as a divine decree that "adopts some to hope of life, and sentences others to eternal death."[41] Calvin's use of the term "predestination" was thus importantly different from his esteemed predecessors. Yet not too much should be made of this fact. This change in terminology makes for a verbal difference between Calvin's views and those of Augustine and Aquinas, but makes little difference to the content of Calvin's theology. The Augustinian tradition had not found a systematic way of speaking about God's overarching plan for creation. Calvin dealt with this problem by speaking of predestination not in the narrow way that Augustine had, always as an act of grace, but more broadly, as an all-embracing decree that encompasses both mercy and justice. In the midst of this shift in terminology Calvin's theology held on to the central elements he had inherited from Augustine. He still distinguished a prevenient order of grace, which he called election, from an order of punishment, which he called reprobation.[42] He did not see these as simply two sides of a coin, but as two different streams of divine action. Thus, he spoke, like Aquinas and Luther, of the reprobate as "those whom God passes over."[43]

Like Luther, Calvin tried not to be the least bit evasive in making the point that those whom God passes over are those whom God wills to exclude. God knows what will happen to creatures God does not actively seek to save, and must intend that outcome and be responsible for it. "It is useless to have recourse here [in the story

of the hardening of Pharaoh's heart] to the concept of permission,"
he wrote, "as if God were said to do what was done only in the
sense that he allowed it."[44] Calvin's rejection of the language of
permission in relation to reprobation does not, however, mean that
he thought God elected and reprobated in the same way, causally.
Calvin consistently recognized a distinction in the way God causally relates to salvation (by giving grace) and damnation (by leaving
sinners to their sin). His point was that this distinction should not
be taken to amount to mere permission, as if God had not planned
for this state of affairs from the start but was merely dealing with
things as they happened. It is not as though the reprobate have a
libertarian freedom while the elect have a compatibilist freedom.
Both lie under the divine determination.

In making this point, Calvin repeatedly linked his understanding
of created ontology to his soteriology. If Augustine had been right to
claim that we cannot bring into being anything good that is merely
our own (and not from God), then those who do not receive grace
will be unfit for eternal life.[45] Calvin thus embraced Luther's argument that a positive doctrine of election conceptually implies the
privation of reprobation. For God to make a decree regarding the
former is, implicitly if not explicitly, to make a decree regarding
the latter as well. For example, if God does not give Pharaoh the
help necessary for his heart to change, he will be hardened against
God's people, and this must be in some sense intended by God.
Endorsing this Augustinian truism did not, however, lead Calvin to
claim that God is the sole cause of all things, or that election and
reprobation are enacted via the same causal order.

In keeping with this line of thought, Calvin affirmed that God
is the primary active agent of all of human history; humans are
important agents but also clearly secondary. It is misleading, he
argued, to imply that God sometimes sits passively by, watching
events unfold (especially those central to salvation history). This
claim was especially important for Calvin because he was willing to
accept Anselm's view that divine foreknowledge "imposes no necessity upon creatures."[46] He accepted that view, however, because he
considered it pointless to argue about the implications of foreknowledge when theologians ought to affirm on independent grounds
that "all things take place by [God's] determination and bidding."[47]
Thus, Calvin explicitly accepted Luther's adherence to divine determinism. He wrote that "the will of God is the chief and principle

cause of all things."[48] It is therefore "proper for us to regard the order of nature as divinely determined."[49] Calvin clarified that a proper theological doctrine of divine determinism differs from what he called "the necessity of Stoicism."[50] His view was not that we are ruled by a chain of causes, or an indifferent fate, but by a divine will that acts with intent, both justly and mercifully.

Calvin did not offer the caveats about how divine determinism might not apply to "lower things" that Luther had offered. This makes him the most clear and thoroughgoing proponent of divine determinism we have discussed. Some take this to confirm their belief in the radical and new nature of Calvin's approach to predestination, but it is hard to see how Calvin's consistent determinism makes for particularly significant differences between his view and Luther's. Luther, after all, had both personally embraced a complete determinism and even when making concessions had not allowed for anything morally or spiritually significant to escape divine determination. We might also note that Calvin disagreed with Luther's rejection of the traditional Aristotelian distinction between absolute and contingent necessity (to which we have already seen Anselm and Aquinas refer). Calvin accepted that much of what happens in the created order is contingently necessary—it could have been otherwise, had God willed it.[51] Here again it is hard to see how this difference between Luther and Calvin amounts to anything especially significant. Both authors emphasized that the divine will cannot be thwarted, and their views have similar implications. The differences between their views amount mainly to the fact that Calvin presented his doctrine of predestination in a more systematic manner than Luther had.

If Calvin and Luther's doctrines of double predestination were essentially the same, the same cannot be said of the way they approached the relationship between divine and human agency. Perhaps in response to what seems to already have been widespread concern that Luther's picture of human agency was too passive, Calvin highlighted human agency to a much greater degree—a move that made possible his well-known tendency to emphasize the theme of sanctification more than Luther had. His depiction of human agency was able to be more active because he moved away from Luther's rejection of Aristotle, instead embracing Aquinas and Augustine's desire to offer a more philosophically complex approach to human nature and psychology. As we have seen, Luther had his own rich if often implicit moral psychology, so the difference between Luther and Calvin here should not be overstated. Both theologians took a broadly Augustinian approach that emphasized the noncompetitive relationship between the human and the divine. Nevertheless, the symbolism of Calvin's decision to title his main work on the question of human and divine agency *The Bondage and Liberation of the Will*, contraposed to Luther's *Bondage*, is difficult to ignore.

Perhaps the most obvious difference between them is that whereas Luther wanted to avoid using the (as he considered it) misleading term "free choice," Calvin was more comfortable with the term. Luther would not have taken issue with Calvin's use of the term to describe the power Adam and Eve had to cling to the good before they lost their freedom in the fall.[52] He had, however, resisted making use of the term in a less "royal" sense to apply to the volitional powers of fallen human agents. Calvin, by contrast, offered a definition of the term that allowed it to apply equally to pre- and postlapsarian humanity. "If freedom is opposed to coercion, I both acknowledge and consistently maintain that choice is free," he wrote.[53] On this noncompetitive approach, a choice can be free and determined simultaneously, so long as a person moves of his or her own accord, and is not forcibly moved by an external impulse. As a result, it was possible for Calvin to speak of both sinners and the saved as having free choice even while recognizing that they were determined by the power of sin or, respectively, the power of grace.

In his regular usage, however, Calvin hewed to a line similar to Luther's, because like Luther he found that talking about free choice led listeners to assume that humans have an ability and power that he thought we most assuredly do not have. In addition, he noted both that the scripture speaks of sinners as being in bondage and the paradoxical air of saying that those in bondage have free choice. As a less confusing alternative, he offered the option of calling sinners "self-determined," where, like Aquinas, he had in mind the claim that they are responsible for their acts when and because they act voluntarily, directing themselves in the direction they go rather than being "dragged unwillingly."[54] In support of the claim that actions and good or bad character can be both voluntary and necessary, Calvin particularly cited a theological argument he had found in Augustine and Bernard of Clairvaux. Both had observed that although God is good of necessity, we nonetheless praise God. This is appropriate, they contended, because God's goodness is voluntary.[55]

God's necessary goodness is voluntary, in part, because it is not forced upon him. Calvin explicitly relied on Aristotle for help in making the classic compatibilist distinction between acting out of necessity and being forced in his *Bondage and Liberation of the Will*. "In Aristotle at any rate the existence of alternative possibilities is always the opposite of necessity."[56] So what is necessary is what cannot be otherwise, such as the impossibility of God being other than good. But, he noted, it is possible for an act to be voluntary even if it cannot be otherwise. God, for instance, is good because God wills to be. Thus, the voluntary and the necessary may coincide.

In applying these ideas to human behavior, Calvin had conditions of both grace and sin in mind. In those who receive sanctifying grace, God (who as we will see Calvin considered neither external to sinners nor a forcer of their wills) moves so that they make determinate choices that are free. Prior to receiving divine grace, fallen human beings experience sin as both voluntary and necessary. It is voluntary because it finds its source in the internal agential capacities of the sinful person him or herself. It is necessary because after the fall human nature is corrupted, having developed a "habit" of evil willing.

Here some clarification is required so that we do not misread Calvin. For Calvin this "habit" of human nature is a product of original sin, with which postlapsarian humanity is born. As a result, Calvin was not using the term "habit" as we typically now do, to refer to a refined power for action that is developed with effort over time. Rather, he used the term in the traditional Aristotelian sense, meaning something similar to what we sometimes call a "habitus," or a formation of a way of being. The fallen nature of original sinners means that their impulses will ultimately be twisted in evil ways, and thus they act under a kind of necessity, albeit one engendered by their own twisted powers of loving and knowing.

At times Calvin infamously made it sound as though there is nothing good left in fallen humanity. He wrote, for instance, that "from God they are good, but from themselves they are evil."[57] He clarified his view, however, by explaining (again, depending more heavily on Aristotle than we have been led to expect) that reasoning and will are both defective after the fall, not in their essential substance but in their accidental qualities.[58] This defective state creates in humanity a new "natural" inclination to corruption, one that is not in fact entirely natural to us, since human nature is good as established by God, and only secondarily bad. It is this contrast between created and inherited qualities of nature that makes the metaphor of enslavement by sin appropriate. On Calvin's view we have by created nature the ability to will, which cannot be taken away from us. However, the will is like prime matter, ready to receive form.[59] By creation it had a good form. Grace allows it to put on another and better form, but the natural depravity of bondage to sin gives it a bad form unless God liberates it.

These philosophical clarifications made it possible for Calvin to explain and defend some of the more controversial aspects of his theology of predestination. As we have just seen, he often stated, quoting or paraphrasing Augustine, that we have nothing of our own but sin. Read in isolation, such a statement sounds unduly harsh, and foolish as well, since it seems clear that even sinners can be reasonably good friends, loving parents, and so on. Calvin clarified, however, that in this context the Augustinian claim he was retrieving refers to what we have in ourselves, apart from God's gracious action in creation and redemption. What we have simply of ourselves is not the good, because having the good always depends on divine activity, which is the sole independent generator of the good. Sin and evil, by contrast, are not generated by God even though they are incorporated into God's plan and decree. What we contribute to the world on our own, then, is only sin and evil. The inescapable conclusion is that we are meant to be co-operating agents, not autonomous.

Evil is not all we contribute to the world, because by grace even fallen wills are liberated from their bondage to sin. Sanctifying grace makes it possible for created agents to be causes of good in their own right, as dependent causes. As we have seen, God draws sinners to the good in a manner that cannot be resisted, but not by force. God draws sinners willingly because God is able to make sinful wills anew. God does not make sinners act against their wills, but gives their willing a new form.[60] Sanctified goodness, too, can therefore be both voluntary and necessary. When the defective aspects of human powers of reasoning and ability to will are repaired, the sanctified cannot do otherwise than good, but since that is also what they want to do they act voluntarily.

This understanding of the relationship between human and divine agency led Calvin to insist on the importance of keeping in mind what he called the diversity of causes. Echoing Aquinas's distinction between primary and secondary causes, though using different language, Calvin argued that although God is the remote cause of what comes to pass, we are often significant proximate causes.[61] Many earthly events happen or fail to happen because of what human beings will. Pastoral exhortation and civic punishment recognize this fact. Calvin's determinism has at times been thought to make attempts to reform or blame, or to encourage others, pointless. If people are going to do what they will do, regardless, why bother trying to intervene? In response, Calvin argued that God may have ordained a person to be motivated to do something after being rebuked, punished, or reacted to in some other way. In order to involve us in the divine plan, God has prescribed that many things will come to pass only by our taking proper care in doing them. Determinism, therefore, may incorporate the importance of practices of blame, punishment, reward, and praise within its logic.

Given what we have seen Calvin say, it should be clear by now that he held sinners blameworthy for evil when they are not forced but act voluntarily, even if they cannot do or be otherwise. This makes sense, on his view, because what is self-determined (in his compatibilist sense of that term) should be attributed to that person. To give a simple example, let us say that I harm you because that is what I want to do, for whatever good or bad reasons I think I have. Calvin did not think it should make a difference to our assessment of my responsibility for that action if we learned that (given divine foreknowledge, and my character, and so on) I could not have done otherwise. What matters, in his view, is not what I might have done had the world been different but who I actually am in the real world.[62]

What can seem surprisingly severe and inconsistent is that Calvin was reluctant to make the obvious parallel point that human beings should also be credited for their merits. Once again, however, it is important not to overreact and draw too many conclusions. Calvin's reluctance to attribute praise was mainly rhetorical in nature. Calvin did not consider sanctified (or even simply sinful) creaturely agents entirely undeserving of commendation, or lacking in merit.

Rather, he took the pastoral approach that it is dangerous to talk us up too much. Like Augustine, but even more so, he worried that giving human beings much credit makes it all too easy for them to forget their fundamentally dependent status and situation. We are, he thought, all too ready to be overly confident in our abilities and wisdom. Because fallen human beings are so eager to believe in the efficacy and rightness of their actions, he wanted to emphasize by contrast that God always deserves the primary credit for being good. Human goodness is real but it is also secondary at best. This invitation to humility was a tactic that Calvin sometimes took too far. Still, that was a flaw less in his account of responsibility than in its rhetorical application.

In closing, it is natural to wonder how Calvin was able to maintain his insistence on the unimpeachability of divine goodness, given that he also insisted on the activity of divine agency in what are for human beings sinful actions. To take the classic case, why is it a sin for Pharaoh to keep the children of Israel enslaved but not a sin for the God who is, in one way or another, determining Pharaoh's actions? Calvin's responses to this problem very often echoed those we heard from Luther and others before him. God cannot do wrong, and at any rate what position are we in to judge? His ways are higher than ours.

More explicitly than his predecessors, Calvin also advanced a further argument about how God can be the cause of all that happens and yet not an author of evil. For Calvin, God is like the author of a story in which some bad things happen.[63] In his view, the mere existence of those evils in the author's story is not enough to taint the author. If God's intentions in telling the story that is told in creation and its subsequent history were impure in some way, then God could be blamed. However, since God always intends good in whatever God does, Calvin suggested that God cannot be said to be doing evil even when God intends an action to happen that is, for its human agent, evil. God can thereby cooperate in the doing of a deed that is evil for the human agent but not for God. Some of Calvin's comments on this idea can sound reminiscent of Peter Abelard's controversial claim that intention fully determines the moral worth of an action, but that was not Calvin's view. His many discussions of human sin make it clear that he thought sinners can be blameworthy even when they have good intentions.[64] Because fallen human natures are flawed, human agents can will ill without realizing it. Moreover, because of ignorance, good intentions do not always protect fallen human beings from doing wrong. For God, however, whose omniscience Calvin took for granted, good intentions are enough. We may wonder how God could countenance some of the horrors of history without evil intent, but that question returns us to the mystery of the divine plan. Scripture gives occasional glimpses of the complexity of the divine will, such as Joseph's famous statement that what his brothers who sold him into slavery meant for evil, God had meant for good (Gen 50:20). But in general Calvin did not pretend to have answers to everyday questions about why particular evils come to pass, or how a good God could justify having brought about this world in which those evils exist.

Calvin recognized that doctrines of reprobation can sound heartless. At one point he even called the divine decree "dreadful indeed, I confess."[65] He was keen, however, to submit his teaching to what he took to be the clear message of the Bible and of the Augustinian tradition. He did not see how we could find fault with God, who is merciful in graciously saving some who do not deserve such mercy, and just in condemning others whose sin is self-determined. Moreover, he believed that his teaching about predestination, providence, and divine determinism did not make questions about the goodness and grandeur of God any more difficult than they already are on weaker views, like that of Anselm or Calvin's own libertarian theological opponents. On the contrary, he found that on the whole these doctrines add a sense of reassurance. In spite of the many things we do not understand, they make it possible to affirm with confidence that God is ultimately in charge, that the victory won in Jesus Christ cannot be wasted, and that the ultimate history of creation is and will be good.

5

Barth's hopeful universalism

It has often been said that the heart of Calvin's theology was his doctrine of predestination. Most scholars now consider that claim more true of the Reformed orthodoxy that came after Calvin than of Calvin himself (his main theme may have been union with Christ). Karl Barth, however, explicitly and even pointedly made his innovative doctrine of election the most exhaustively discussed central theme in his massive *Church Dogmatics*. "The election of grace is the sum of the Gospel... But more, the election of grace is the whole of the Gospel, the Gospel in *nuce*," he wrote.[1] He emphasized this point by making a lengthy exploration of predestination the capstone of his doctrine of God, and then revisiting his doctrine of election throughout his *Dogmatics*, particularly in his discussions of providence and vocation.

What made his doctrine of predestination a radical shift from the Augustinian tradition was not simply its location in his systematic theology but the content he gave it. That content was signaled by Barth's decision to call his doctrine of predestination a doctrine of election. Here he paid homage to Calvin's use of the term "predestined" while significantly reorienting it. Calvin, of course, had thought of election as the positive side of a divine predestining that includes also a "No" to those who are reprobate. For Barth, however, predestination is best understood as "the election of grace" because in the end God's "Yes" to all is more powerful and characteristic than any "No." Indeed, Barth argued, what we know in Christ is that any "No" is said only for the sake of a greater and finally determinative "Yes." Election is not merely one side of divine predestination, therefore, but the whole of it. It will immediately sound as though Barth was defending universalism. Yet what he offered was deliberately not a *doctrine* of universalism, but rather a thesis about the logic of Christian faith that necessarily leads to a hope for universal salvation. That hope, however, remains uncertain until the end of all things. In turn, that uncertainty raises interesting questions about the relationship between divine and human agency on Barth's view.

1. The problem of assurance

Barth's unorthodox doctrine of election was motivated by two correlated criticisms of all the Augustinian doctrines of predestination that had come before him. Put positively, his criticism was that previous doctrines of predestination had failed to base their claims sufficiently on Christ. Put negatively, his criticism was that previous doctrines of predestination had trapped believers in an endless cycle of anxiety about whether they were among God's elect. These two concerns were connected by his charge that predestination had traditionally made too much of the deeply mysterious nature of the divine decrees concerning the ultimate destiny of each person. For these reasons, far from bringing the reassurance of God's grace that the Reformers had intended, the doctrine had created fear. "All the earnest statements concerning the majesty and mystery of God, all the well-meaning protestations of His fatherly loving-kindness, cannot in any way alter the fact that we necessarily remain anxious in respect of our election."[2]

Where, after all, were believers to look for reassurance? Clearly, it is not especially reassuring to simply know that God is powerful and good to some. One would like to know whether God has grace for me, and for those I care about. Augustine and his followers had always said that Christians should hold by faith to the assurance that God is for us and not against us. But the tenuous nature of this assurance could be seen in the endless arguments about reassurance provoked by the doctrine of predestination, not least in Reformed and Puritan circles. Some proposed that the elect could see signs of their status inside the circle of God's grace by looking to themselves and their own works. The elect, after all, are supposed to be sanctified. Yet as Luther had found, it is doubtful that in this life

Christians can look to themselves to ascertain whether and how they are beloved of God. Both he and Calvin had strongly warned against attempts to do so.[3] A foolish and blind conscience might consider oneself to be quite mature. A humble and sensitive conscience is likely to see all manner of fault in oneself, where others would see mainly virtue. Moreover, as Barth often noted, sensitive consciences are right to be concerned, because all fall short. Until God is all in all, the Christian life is a mixture of genuine witness to God's glory and to the ongoing power of sin. Even if Christians are better than they would have been without God's call in their lives they may not look all that good when compared to the many upstanding citizens who are at least apparently outside the church. Human experience permits no unequivocal marks of election or rejection by God, Barth argued.[4] It is worth noting that his point would have force even if softened, since even if there are a few decisive marks of election or reprobation they are too rare in human experience to be of any help to the vast majority of people.

For these reasons, among others, it seems clear that trust in God's election should be based not on looking to oneself but on looking to Christ. Calvin, of course, had said just this, as had Luther. Barth's concern, however, was that merely looking to Christ is not enough, so long as it is possible to fear that his call is issued to others but not to oneself. If we are balanced between the possibilities of election and reprobation the doctrine of predestination is not a doctrine of grace but a doctrine of ultimate uncertainty. Barth feared that, ultimately, the Augustinian tradition had found the theological basis for the doctrine of election in what he called a *decretum absolutum*, a mysterious decree that can be given no theological logic but only referred to an arbitrary, voluntarist divine will. The idea that a doctrine so central to the gospel should be referred to a hidden, unknowable and unpredictable God is, Barth stated, idolatrous.[5] Thus, in order to recover and make good on Augustine's conviction that predestination is a matter of grace, founded in Christ, Barth made a radical proposal.

According to Barth's doctrine of election, God does not elect individual human beings directly, choosing some and perhaps ignoring others. Rather, God himself is the primary object of divine election.[6] In making this claim, Barth appropriated Augustine's view that in the predestination of Christ we see what predestination is—but took it in a direction Augustine could not have foreseen.

For Barth, Jesus is not merely the best example of predestination but the one in whom election primarily takes place. In and through him, and for his sake, all of humanity is elect. He is also the one who was damned, and rejected by God. Indeed, Christ contains in himself the damnation of all, since he took upon himself the sin of all. Yet in Christ the logic of reprobation is revealed to be penultimate. Christ became one who was despised and rejected for our sake, that we might be accepted by God, and not rejected. The ultimate logic of predestination, therefore, is that "from all eternity God has determined upon man's acquittal at His own cost."[7] "Predestination is the non-rejection of man...because it is the rejection of the Son of God."[8] This, Barth suggested, is a new kind of doctrine of double predestination, in which from all eternity God elected fellowship with humanity for Himself and fellowship with Himself for humanity.[9]

2. Christ the center

The obvious questions that this doctrine raises about the status of hell in Christian theology have tended to overshadow other important elements of Barth's doctrine of election. We should ask not just about the potentially universalistic implications of Barth's Christological transformation of the doctrine of predestination but, first of all, why Barth put Christ so thoroughly at the center of all human history. The answer to this latter question is tied up with Barth's understanding of the meaning of human history, and his associated "supralapsarian" approach to predestination.[10]

Augustine's approach to predestination, and that of most of his followers, had been "infralapsarian," in the sense that he typically spoke as if God had decided to create, foreseen the fall, and then decided to respond to this by predestining some to be saved through Jesus Christ. On this way of thinking the incarnation is a great good, intended by God as a cure for sin that would not have happened had the Fall not happened. This does not mean that Augustine thought of the incarnation as an accidental feature of creation. Because God foreknew the Fall and how he would respond to it, God intended the incarnation from the beginning, and may have even permitted the Fall in order to make possible the great good of redemption via unity with Christ. This chain of thought led to the idea of the Fall as a potentially "happy fault," which was an important part of Augustine's response to the problem of evil. The main point for our purpose here, however, is that Augustine's approach to the incarnation made it conceptually dependent on the Fall and sin.

On Barth's supralapsarian view, by contrast, God planned the incarnation for its own sake. As a result, the incarnation is not a response to sin; rather, all of creation and its history exist to make the incarnation possible. God first thought of Jesus Christ, and thus of God and humanity together. Creation followed after, as the necessary concomitant. As Barth put it, "in predestination it is a matter primarily and properly of the eternal election of the Son of God to be the Head of His community and of all creatures. ...the eternal decree...does not presuppose the act of creation and the existence of creatures but is itself their presupposition."[11] God's eternal plan, as Barth described it, began with the election of God to be man, and man to be with God, in Jesus Christ. That is the goal of history, and the purpose of creation.

In order to reinforce his point about the priority and centrality of the doctrine of predestination, Barth positioned his doctrine of election at the conclusion of his doctrine of God in the *Dogmatics* and prior to his discussions of providence and salvation. Locating his discussion there, as a fitting capstone to the discussion of God's nature and activity, reinforced Barth's argument that both God's stance toward the world and our knowledge of God depend on divine election. God as we know him is God for us, given to us in Christ. As we have seen, one of Barth's great concerns about the Augustinian tradition was what he considered its dangerous willingness to speculate about God on some basis other than Christ. Barth insisted that theology can only be on a firm footing if it attends to what God has given us to believe, and he often reminded his readers that the God we have been given to believe in is the God of the election of grace, the God of Jesus Christ.[12]

Barth agreed with Luther and Calvin, of course, that the doctrine of the election of grace is also the sum of Christian soteriology. He also agreed with Aquinas that there is a deep relationship between the doctrines of predestination and providence. However, he wanted to emphasize that the relationship in both cases is one in which predestination is prior. God rules providentially in order that God's eternal plan may be effected in the course of human history. Providence is thus for the sake of predestination, which makes it misleading to call predestination an aspect of God's providence. Similarly, God redeems so that the election of Christ might be fulfilled. Soteriology is thus the fulfillment of a plan decreed long before salvation came to pass.

Given these commitments, Barth told the story of creation this way:

> In the beginning...before creation, before there was any reality distinct from God which be the object of the love of God or the setting for His acts of freedom, God anticipated and determined within Himself...that the goal and meaning of all His dealings with the as yet non-existent universe should be the fact that in His Son He would be gracious towards man, uniting Himself with him.[13]

Traditional theologies of Creation, like Augustine's, typically thought of the first created man, Adam, as the characteristic human being, the template of and source for all the rest of humanity. Barth, however, considered Adam secondary, and Christ primary.[14] Naturally, this raises questions about Barth's Christology, which I will attempt to touch on here only insofar as they illume his doctrine of election.

One of the more striking puzzles of Barth's discussion of Christ as the one who is both electing and elected concerns the way he often spoke as though Jesus was already present prior to Creation—as if he (and not simply the Son) were a member of the Trinity. Barth wrote, for instance, that "It is by Him, Jesus Christ, and for Him and with Him, that the universe was created..."[15] It would be quite odd if he meant to claim that the Jewish carpenter Jesus was temporally at the beginning of the universe. That view would not even make sense, since it would put Barth in the position of claiming that a human person existed prior to the creation of humanity. Such statements are less confusing, however, once we attend to the fact that Barth was intentionally echoing the sometimes mysterious but similar statements made in the Bible. The New Testament often speaks of humanity as predestined through and created by Christ—and even of the Lamb of God as having been "slain before the foundation of the world."[16] These passages are not simply referring to the activity of the Son, the second person of the Trinity. Barth followed the New Testament in speaking of these before-the-world-was-born activities as having been done through Jesus, the historical person in whom God and humanity were united, and who had called the apostles.[17]

What, then, might Barth have had in mind when appropriating this biblical language attesting to Christ's prevenience? According to Barth's view, the primacy of Jesus Christ was not historical, in an embodied sense. Adam (or the humanity Adam represents) was created first in time. What came before Adam was God's election of all humanity, including Adam, in the divine choice to create Jesus. And, Barth indicated, it is appropriate to speak of Jesus as being prior to Creation in this sense: "Jesus Christ was the choice or election of God."[18] "The one Jesus Christ, who is as such of both divine and human essence...preexisted as such in the divine counsel."[19] In other words, Jesus Christ was first, conceptually and ontologically. He has conceptual primacy because God thought first not of a generic humanity but of a specific person, in whom humanity was united with himself. The first human being in God's plan was Jesus, who provides the pattern for all the rest of humanity. He has ontological primacy because God covenanted with Godself and with the yet to be incarnate God-man that all human nature would come to be for his sake, and thus through him. Indeed, Barth argued that all human persons partake of Christ's humanity, and are therefore "in" Christ in a strong sense. "The human nature elected by Him and assumed into unity with His existence is implicitly that of all men. In His being as man God has implicitly assumed the human being of all men."[20]

The ontological priority of Jesus meant, for Barth, that the historical person Jesus of Nazareth was not only a particular individual, in whom the divine Son and a particular human nature were united, but also the source of all humanity. That is how it was possible for God to elect all in electing this one. To be clear, Barth did not view the human nature that was united with the Triune God in the person of Jesus as generic, a general "all humanity." Jesus Christ was not some vague combination of universals, God and humanity as such. He was the Son united with an individual human nature. Because that human nature was the basis for all the rest of humanity, however, it has a universal significance. "Jesus of Nazareth was and is a man as we are—our Brother. But he was and is our first-born Brother. As a man like all men, He was and is the head of all men."[21]

That God elects Jesus, and all of humanity in him, to be in relationship with the divine is no surprise, on Barth's account, because in making Christ the center of God's creative activity God is simply being Godself. Barth reflected throughout the *Dogmatics* on the Christian affirmation that God is love. It is God's nature to love because God is Triune. What it, therefore, means for God to be God, above all, is to live in loving community.[22] That God is Father, Son, and Spirit means that the divine life is not one of solitude but of fellowship and sharing. Consequently, love is a necessary feature of the divine life. Barth clarified that this necessity is not imposed by some external power or rule. Love is necessary to God in the sense that it is key to God's identity, so much so that God is identified with love. The fact that God is love is essential to Barth's conception of predestination as a covenant of grace.

Divine love explains, though it does not make necessary, God's decision to create for the sake of bringing what is and is not divine into relationship. As Barth liked to express the point, a covenant of love is the internal basis of Creation, since the covenant is that which motivates God to create and gives Creation its logic. Conversely, Creation is the external basis of the covenant. Creation of that which is not divine makes the covenant possible, and indeed, actual.[23] In developing this theme of the correspondence between Creation and covenant, Barth made good use of an image important to Augustine, the idea of love as an overflowing fountain. Election, creation, providence, salvation, eschatological consummation—and even, as we will see, a certain relationship of created things to evil— all express the divine plenitude, the joy God has in sharing God's life with others. God does not need to share, but it makes sense for God to do so.

Indeed, it makes so much sense that it becomes difficult to imagine what else God might have done, given who God has shown himself to be. Our difficulty in imagining God otherwise might, on Barth's view, result from the limitations of our imaginations, and the limitations of our ability to know God. It is fitting, however, that we can only imagine God this way, because God is now, contingently but necessarily, committed to being this God, the God of Jesus Christ, God for us. As we saw when introduced to Barth's redescription of the idea of "double predestination" above, election not only constitutes those who are elected, it also has a (limited but real and significant) power to constitute the elector. In electing humanity for relationship with God, God also elects Godself for relationship with humanity.

3. Liberated to obey

Because election means God's gift of himself to us, the God who elects is, as Barth eloquently put it, "both benefactor and benefit."[24] Barth's teaching that predestination means first and foremost the election of Jesus Christ, and therefore of God for us and us for God, was novel. However, as he developed the claim that God elects a certain mutuality between God and humanity, he did not abandon the traditional view that predestination also means divine sovereignty. The covenant bestowed in Creation is not ratified by equals, but rather decreed by the creator. Accordingly, Barth emphasized that God is prior, the one whose plan and action is the basis for all of our actions and plans. It is in this sense, Barth wrote, that the electing God rules. God rules not as some "irresistibly efficacious power *in abstracto*, naked freedom and sovereignty as it were," but as the God of Jesus Christ, a personal being who intends and loves.[25] The doctrine of predestination teaches that the Triune God rules, and not mere determinism or indeterminism.

Barth's claim that God rules and not determinism had a number of important implications. One we have just discussed—God's plan for the world is not logically necessary, a story that had to be told. Election, like Creation itself, is contingent, since God presumably could have told a different story in the history of this or some other world. Having chosen this plan, however, God is committed to it, and it does not change or falter. It is, therefore, contingently necessary. Here it is useful to keep in mind Luther's reminder that for practical purposes "contingently necessary" simply means necessary, from the point of view of our experience.

But necessary in what way? Like Calvin, who rejected Stoic conceptions of fate, Barth emphasized that the events of world history are not blind or indifferent. Rather, they are ever guided by God's intentions, which have at their center a *telos*, Jesus Christ. The plan that God is enacting is not mechanistic, a series of causes started at some point in the past by a distant deity. The world remains under God's personal care. Thus, a properly theological account of predestination teaches that the God who rules does not control human beings as involuntary puppets or slaves, coerced by the divine will.[26] Jesus, who in his human nature was not forced into obedience, offers a central example of Barth's point. "He speaks of His suffering, not as a necessity laid upon Him from without, but as something which He Himself wills... In His wholehearted obedience, in His electing of God alone, He is wholly free."[27]

Perhaps because Barth (like Luther) wanted to avoid letting philosophy set the direction for his theology, he did not carefully clarify the meaning of some of the key terms he used in discussing the relationship between divine and human agency. He affirmed God's personal and caring sovereignty, but also at times juxtaposed that theme with the idea that human beings have autonomy. It is understandable, therefore, that Barth's claim that Jesus was "wholly free" has led some readers to wonder if Jesus could have disobeyed God's call, rejected his suffering and his salvific mission, and listened to Peter's argument that he should run from death.

At times, Barth spoke of both divine and human freedom in ways that could sound radically libertarian. Reading Barth this way is especially plausible in relation to some of his comments about divine freedom, where Barth opened himself to being read as a libertarian by stating that God is "One who wills Himself," whose "being is decision," and claiming that God is unique in that "No other being is absolutely its own, conscious, willed and executed decision."[28] Taken in isolation, these statements might seem to imply the radical idea that God's decision to be with us in Christ is the basis of the Trinity—which would make election prior to the creation not only of creatures but also of God himself, as we know him. Similarly, Barth sometimes spoke strongly of humans as possessing a "simple but comprehensive autonomy" and of human agency as "spontaneous," both of which can make it sound as though human action is fundamentally unconstrained, a power unto itself.[29] Again, such statements might seem to imply a strong libertarian theme in Barth's view of human agency, one that suggests that Jesus, in his autonomy, could have chosen to disobey the Father and thus to have thwarted God's entire plan for creation.

The very radicality of these possibilities gives us reason to be suspicious of readings that make Barth out to be a libertarian, however. It is wise to guard against letting our cultural proclivity toward libertarian conceptions of freedom color our assumptions about what some of the terms Barth used must have meant. When Barth disagreed with traditional Christian views, he typically discussed why directly and openly. So we should be especially careful about taking him to have had hyperlibertarian views given the fact that he never explicitly indicated his intent to make such a strong break from the traditions on which he drew. Perhaps inevitably for one who wrote as quickly as he did, Barth made unguarded and puzzling statements, some of which may be impossible to integrate into a single coherent view. Nonetheless, there are persistent, central themes in the *Dogmatics* that resist a libertarian reading, and which would be made incoherent by such an approach. Barth's conviction that divine election is sure stands out, but it is far from alone.

On the whole, Barth's discussion of human and divine freedom was distinctly nonlibertarian. As we will see, Barth denigrated the import of choice while highlighting God's definite rule over history and the dependent nature of human agency. This is not to say that Barth was a philosophical compatibilist. Barth's views are, philosophically speaking, too underdeveloped for such a claim to make sense. Moreover, it is not clear that Barth drew on Augustine's compatibilism in the way we have seen that Aquinas, Luther, and Calvin did. At the same time, given what he wanted to say about election, freedom, and human and divine agency, a compatibilist approach similar to the views articulated by those theologians would have been the best way for Barth to make his theological convictions coherent and plausible.

This point holds because, in spite of Barth's clear and important differences from Augustine concerning the Christ-centered nature of election, there are significant similarities in the two theologians' accounts of predestination as prevenient grace. After all, both agreed, in opposition to Anselm, that predestination is not simply a matter of divine foreknowledge, where God chooses those who choose God (indeed, both theologians interpreted divine foreknowledge in light of predestination, so that what God knows is what God wills and what God does).[30] Rather, election is (as Barth said of Christian vocation), "the eminently real determination of all humanity by the supreme reality of the divine act of salvation for and to it and the living divine Word..."[31] For Augustine the scope of the divine determination of grace was smaller, but it nevertheless had the character that Barth described. God destines the elect for a place in the Triune life, and accordingly gives those who are in Christ a gift of prevenient grace that human agency has no basis to reject but can only accept. That is because human willing is entirely dependent on the divine will, never separate from it. Thus, although God, by the power of the Spirit, sets Christians on their own feet, the Christian must always affirm that "I cannot take a single step alone."[32]

Closely associated with this theme of the sure divine determination of God's electing grace is the association Barth consistently highlighted between creaturely freedom and obedience. Like Augustine, Barth emphasized that human freedom is fundamentally dependent and directed, an asymmetrical ability to say "Yes" to God even though one cannot say "No." He wrote, for instance, "That [the creature] is elected by the grace of God means also, then, that he too becomes free... Our return to obedience is indeed the aim of free grace. It is for this that it makes us free."[33] Similarly, he argued later in the *Dogmatics* that "the creature has no freedom but that which is grounded on the unconditioned and irresistible freedom and supremacy of God, having no power to concur but only to corroborate and understand and glorify."[34]

Barth's point was that human freedom, like the electoral decree that makes it possible, has a definite logic and goal. God elects to give creaturely persons a limited individuality and autonomy that befits them. This agency is given not for its own sake, however, but so that humanity might elect God in return. Barth therefore shared Augustine and Luther's normative conception of freedom as having a relational *telos*. In Christ God liberates humanity not for the sake of a general or abstract freedom but for a very particular one. The point of election is not just to empower humanity to live some kind of life but to bestow the true life God has. Outside of that life humanity is not truly free.

Although Barth particularly highlighted a normative conception in his discussions of freedom, he also used the idea of freedom in other ways. As noted above, his discussion of freedom sounded most libertarian when he highlighted God's freedom from the control of or obligation to other powers. We have seen his insistence that God is not compelled to create, and that God does not owe creatures salvation. Such statements might seem to draw on a purely negative view of divine freedom, but, he clarified,

Freedom is, of course, more than the absence of limits, restrictions, or conditions. This is only its negative and to that extent improper aspect—improper to the extent that from this point of view it requires another, at least in so far as its freedom lies in its independence of this other. But freedom in its positive and proper qualities means to be grounded in one's own being, to be determined and moved by oneself. This is the freedom of the divine life and love. In this positive freedom of His, God is also unlimited, unrestricted, and unconditioned from without.[35]

Thus Barth argued that even what might look like a "negative" freedom of God is more fundamentally grounded in a positive freedom, a freedom for life, the freedom to be what one is. For God this means a freedom for blessedness, grace, joy, and not for infelicity or evil. To ask why God's freedom has this particular shape or takes this particular direction is both misleading and inappropriate. As we have seen, for Barth, the God we are given to know in Jesus Christ is the starting point of theology. To ask if God could have been something other than the Triune God who is for us in Jesus Christ would be sheer speculation, a call to seek a God behind the God given to us. Practically speaking, therefore, theology must not require that God could have been otherwise. Rather, it should begin with the actuality of the God of love who is.[36] This God is free, a theological conviction much deeper than any preconceived notion that freedom requires alternate possibilities.

Analogous points hold for Barth's conception of human freedom. The fundamental form of our freedom is not negative, a freedom from compulsion, or political, a freedom to choose this or that, but once again a kind of ontological freedom, a freedom to be who we are. "The only freedom that means something is the freedom to be myself as I was created by God. God did not create a neutral creature, but His creature."[37] This true and significant freedom is pointedly not a freedom to be the ultimate arbiter of one's own status by independently choosing between good or evil. Barth must have had a view like Anselm's in mind when he argued that "the view is inadequate that God's possibility here consists in what can only be called a magical infusion of supernatural powers by whose proper use man can do what he cannot do by his own strength, namely be faithful again to the faithful God."[38] In fact, Barth not only thought of such views as inadequate but as downright pagan. He liked to invoke a famous painting of Hercules, standing indecisively at a crossroads, to illustrate his point.[39] A pagan might think that true freedom lies in undetermined choice between alternate paths, but as we have seen a Christian conception of freedom is not neutral but normative, a freedom for the straight and narrow path. Barth was even willing to go so far as to claim that "Being a slave of Christ means being free."[40]

Barth only sometimes used the paradoxical master–slave, freedom–bondage imagery Luther and Augustine had made central to their rhetoric, but the fact that he used it at all cannot help but raise questions about the nature of human agency on his account. Our discussion so far indicates that whatever he meant in using opaque terms like "autonomy" or "spontaneous" in referring to human agency, Barth was not attracted to a libertarian answer to the question of how divine and human agency relate. Unlike Anselm or other libertarians, who tie human responsibility to an ability to choose among alternatives, Barth insisted that Jesus was free (and therefore responsible) even while lacking any alternative to doing and being what was granted by the divine will. "Who has the initiative in this relationship? Who has the precedence? Who decides? Who rules? God, always God.... All that man can and will do is to pray, to follow, and to obey."[41] Similarly, Barth wrote of the elect that "Because God awakens him to this freedom, he has no other freedom. He has thus no other option but to...will and achieve that for which he is elected..."[42] On this basis, Barth spoke of divine election as irresistible.[43] "If a man has not been allowed to fall by God, then he cannot fall at all, and least of all can he cause himself to fall."[44] According to Barth's view, divine determination and human freedom are clearly compatible.

More than this is difficult to say. Barth's positive view is difficult to describe because he resisted developing any theory that went beyond his core affirmation holding together divine rule and genuine human agency. For instance, in order to further explain the relationship between divine and human action, Barth considered endorsing Aquinas's distinction between primary and secondary causes. However, he held back because he worried that these terms imply an inappropriate similarity between divine and human agency that reduces both to being causes among other causes.[45] God, he insisted, does not compete with human agency. That makes it possible for God to act in what human persons do, without one infringing on the other.

This point brings us to Barth's clearest positive theme, the compatibility of divine and human agency. Barth characteristically developed that theme by elaborating on the ordered cooperation between the divine and human made possible in and by Christ:

> That Christ is in the Christian, has the further meaning that Christ speaks, acts, and rules—and this is the grace of his calling of this man... He takes possession of his free human heart. He rules and controls in the obedience of his free reason. As a divine person it is very possible for Him to do this in the unrestricted sovereignty proper to Himself and yet in such a way that there can be no question whatever of any competition between His person and that of the Christian.[46]

This passage offers an example of Barth's influential claim that there is no competition between divine and human agency. It is notable that Barth does not argue that God cannot or does not determine creaturely activity. Barth did, as we have seen, reject any suggestion that God imposes external necessities on human agency. However, it is essential to keep in mind that Barth's rejection of that sort of determinism—which he seems to have understood as implying a mechanistic order of causes—did not rule out more subtle and theologically suitable forms of determination. As Barth stated, God not only rules but also controls his creatures from within, by reorienting their hearts and minds. This does not happen in a simple causal manner, but divine election creates a clear determination nonetheless. Indeed, without such a determination of the creaturely by the divine it would be hard to have the assurance Barth associated with a proper doctrine of predestination.

For Barth, God's ongoing determination of the creature through election is not at odds with a cooperative relationship, but rather provides the basis of real creaturely agency. Left to our own devices, like the pagan Hercules, we would always choose unbelief. It is an illusion to think that there is freedom—even just freedom of choice—without grace. Fortunately, however, "It is not for man to choose first whether he himself will decide (what an illusion!) for faith or for unbelief."[47] Fortunately, in Christ faith "confronts man as an absolutely superior actuality...the possibility of his unbelief is rejected, destroyed and set aside."[48]

Perhaps not surprisingly, the clearest example of this sort of non-competitive relationship between divine determination and human freedom in obedience is found in Jesus Christ himself. Barth made it clear that Christ's human nature did not elect to be united with the divine Son; it could not do so, because it only exists in that relationship. "The determination of His divine essence is *to* His human [essence], and the determination of His human essence [is] *from* His divine."[49] Barth affirmed that there is a kind of mutuality between Christ's two natures, and a receptivity as well, since the divine nature does not simply impose itself on the human nature. Yet he also insisted that mutuality does not imply a lack of order or a simple equality. The relating of the divine and human in Christ "takes place from above to below first, and only then from below to above."[50] God is elector and in Christ also elected, whereas Jesus' human nature is elected without being, in the first place, elector. Thus, there is an important order of precedence in the relationship between the natures.

Given Christ's role as the firstborn of all creation, the relationship between the divine and human natures in Christ offers an example of the kind of power and activity that, on Barth's view, election always has more generally. God's election of Christ, and in him all humanity, has a creative power because it constitutes the object that is elected. Election is not simply a decision God makes about some existing thing. It is prior to all created existence, and so cannot be an imposition. Consequently, it would be foolish and even strange to want Jesus' human nature to have alternatives to being in Christ. Only in Christ does it exist at all, and only once it is united with the divine nature can it act or consent. At that point, of course, it will say "Yes" to the divine "Yes." Jesus' free obedience is therefore both something he wills and something that is decided by God.

In spite of all Barth's talk about the noncompetitive nature of this relationship, the priority of God's action over human action might seem to make human agency superfluous. What role does human freedom really play if it has all been decided by the electing God and accomplished by the elected God? Barth's answer is that we are needed precisely because the electing God posits us, destining us to be agents who relate to God.

...my life becomes my history—we might almost say my drama—in which I am neither the author nor the producer, but the principal actor. I did not place myself in this movement, nor do I maintain myself in it. But I myself am in this movement. Between my birth and my death the freedom is given to me to be myself in this movement... To be in this freedom is to live.[51]

The electing God elects us to be. The ultimate meaning and nature of our lives is not, Barth maintained, our decision, but is controlled by God, so that we might live in the light of the Word's life, and in so living have the faith and love necessary to share in God's life.

For Barth, obedience to the divine plan is a human choice that could not have been otherwise, for the Christian "has been deprived of all possibilities but one."[52] Human agents are not coerced into taking this one path, but rather determined by their existence in Christ. As Barth explained, the Christian is one who "has awakened from the dream or nightmare of a freedom of choice... It is not external constraint, but his own freedom which he owes to the grace of his Lord electing him in divine freedom, which prevents him from emancipating himself from this Lord."[53] In Christ, humanity has been called to and therefore given a real activity, a significant if subordinate kind of agency. The elect act in faith, and out of love, and therefore act not because God makes them but because of what they want and believe.

Such a life is certainly passive, in that it is fundamentally dependent, a life of response. But that, Barth maintained, is the sort of life suitable for creatures like us. And we do have our own kind of activity, as well. After all, the life for which God elects humanity "does not destroy our intellect and compel us to sacrifice it, but sets it free just as in a definite sense it captivates it, i.e., for itself. It does not break down our will, but sets it in free movement."[54] In this way servitude and liberation can be brought together, and human agency understood both within its proper limits, and as really significant. Barth offered a succinct statement of his view when he wrote, "That [man] is, and is therefore obedient, means that the statement 'I am,' must be interpreted by the further statement: 'I will.' "[55] The limited but genuine agency that pertains to human destinies is both gift and task. Humanity is therefore called to be active.

Like Augustine, Barth considered prayer a fitting summation of the Christian life. For Barth, all of God's commands to humanity fundamentally take the form of a gracious offer: "Call on Me."[56] In this command the God who condemns but also elects and redeems humanity in Christ brings the gospel and law together. What God requires and gives is a life of "invocation of God the Father by humans as his children."[57] A life of invocation is a life of prayer in which the recipients of God's gifts give thanks and praise, offer penitence for their failings, and present their requests. Such a life honors the relationship between divine and human agency, recognizing creaturely limits while affirming the activity suitable to humanity as God's partners. To pray is to remember that it is for God to consummate in their fullness the relationships God elected to create, but also to struggle for reconciliation here and now, because that is the proper mode of witness to the one on whom God's children call.[58] The simple fact that God offers this way of life as the vocation of humanity implies that God wills to defeat evil with our active participation.

In summary, we have seen that Barth's view of human and divine freedom is difficult to clarify because he resisted clarifying it. Even so, a number of significant interrelated themes emerge from his discussions of agency in the light of election. He insisted on the surety of divine predestination. God is sovereign and cannot be thwarted. He also maintained that God's mastery is not competitive with human agency. This is not because God always gives humanity choices but because as creator and redeemer God makes the identities out of which the elect act. For Barth, we do not need to be radically autonomous, the ultimate sources of our being in activity, in order to be free and responsible in our being and activity. Creatures under God's rule are free, in that they are empowered to live the life for which they were created. The juxtaposition of these various claims should not be called a full theory, but when put together they are well fitted to the sort of theory of responsible agency philosophers call compatibilist. It seems appropriate to conclude that Barth could have said what he wanted to say, theologically, more easily and clearly had he developed it with the help of a little more philosophy. Doing so would have helped him avoid the sense, shared by many of his readers, that his view makes human beings too passive.

4. On Judas's fall

An attraction of a libertarian reading of Barth's theology of election is that it offers a straightforward rationale for his resistance to universalism. Perhaps, although God seeks to save the lost, not all can be brought back into the fold. Judas would seem a case in point. He was called, and indeed elected as an apostle, but turned away. In doing so he took his life into his own hands, a point graphically illustrated by his suicide. Barth, however, offered a far more complex interpretation of Judas's story in a lengthy and brilliant small-print excursus at the end of his discussion of election.

Barth began by hinting, if not outright stating, that his exegesis offered not a "plain-sense" reading of individual passages but rather a meditation on the systematic implications and themes of the biblical Judas stories. Two overlapping theological principles guided his discussion. First, he gave any possible benefit of the doubt to the claim, already defended in earlier sections of his treatment of election, that God wills all human beings (and therefore, Judas too!) to exist as the elect, not as the rejected. This he considered a Christological principle, since in Christ we learn that the elect are called for the sake of the nonelect, and that the rejected have no life of their own, over and against the elect.

Second, Barth did of course grant that Judas is among the rejected, at least in a way and for a time. This, however, is a point that Barth understood in the light of his general view of evil. God's purpose in election and Creation, Barth contended, is to call humanity to be witness to God's glory. An aspect of that witness is repudiating that which God repudiates. That, he suggested, is why humanity must confront evil, the defeat of which must occur as an event, in the course of history.[59] For finite beings to turn away from evil we must actually meet it, and come to understand it, within our limits. We must reject it, as God does, participating in God's rejection of it. Barth summed up the implications of these ideas for his treatment of Judas with the following statement:

> His determination is that, as the rejected man which he is, he should hear the proclamation of the truth and come to faith. It is that from being a reluctant and indirect witness he should become a willing and direct witness to the election of Jesus Christ and his community.[60]

Barth considered Judas to be a central example of the place evil and sin have in God's plan and Creation. Indeed, as the greatest sinner of the New Testament, he represents evil and its nature, and in a way even stands in for Satan. Barth thought of evil in general as that which is against the divine will, what God has rejected. To this shadow power Barth gave the name *Das Nichtige* (nothingness). Without going into the complexities of Barth's fascinating but at times obscure account of *Das Nichtige*, it is important to note his conviction that although evil has the character of what is rejected "we may not and cannot say that [evil] is not the object of His will at all; that it escapes His lordship and control."[61] After all, God wills to permit that which is against God's will, if only for a time and in a certain place. In willing to permit evil, God also takes it up into his foreknowledge. There is a sense, therefore, in which it would be right to say that God intends for evil to take place. Barth insisted that God does not will evil in the same manner as the good. Still, he also granted that Luther had been right—it would be misleading to say that God relates to evil simply as a bystander. Divine permission of evil is active and not merely passive. But when we ask why God permits what is rejected to have any place at all, and whether God should be blamed for this, Barth found it essential to appeal to the limits of our understanding. All we can say about why God permits evil, ultimately, is that "If God is greater in the very fact that he is the God who forgives sins and saves from death, we have no right to complain but must praise Him."[62]

Judas, of course, is crucial to the history of redemption that reveals and glorifies God, since he is elected to be the one who betrayed Christ and made his sacrifice for all (not least Judas himself) possible. A key premise of Barth's discussion of Judas is that because he was doing what needed to be done, he was "a planned figure with a planned role" and he was, therefore, a servant of Christ, unable to reject his election but serving it at each point, even as Jesus' betrayer.[63] Because of the role he played, Barth contended, Judas was always "under the direct supervision and control, as it were, of the overruling power and effectiveness of the Lord Himself."[64]

Barth juxtaposed the Bible's sense that Judas did what he must with its portrayal of Judas as reprobate. From himself, of course, Judas perished. Barth grounded that judgment on something more than Matthew's claim that Judas committed suicide. By itself, Judas's suicide might be evidence of a certain sort of good intent. Barth accepted that Judas's death may very well have been an attempt to make amends. He hung himself in remorseful despair. What is damning, on Barth's judgment, is not simply the suicide *per se* but the fact that Judas's very attempt to make amends by killing himself displayed a fundamental misunderstanding of Jesus' life and teaching. In his penitence, Judas attempted to depend on his own work, his own freedom of choice and decision, instead of throwing himself on God's mercy.[65] He thus turned to the law and not the gospel. In doing so, Judas judged himself. In attempting to be his own judge rather than letting the God of grace judge him in and for the sake of Christ, he brought upon himself his own punishment. In *Acts* Judas's death is portrayed as frightful and mysterious—a headlong fall, in which he burst himself asunder. This latter story is not officially a suicide, but it does indicate Judas perished from his own actions. Therefore, Barth suggested, both accounts portray Judas as having, intentionally or unintentionally, done himself in.[66] In Judas's fall, he noted, we have one who has been placed under the sign of the devil, whose end is a picture of hell, in which a person rejects God and is left to his own devices.

Yet Barth was not willing to abandon hope for one whose feet had been washed by Jesus. In Judas's biblical story, he maintained, we have not a final ending but a penultimate one. It would be hasty to give a final answer concerning Judas's fate, because on the one side of the decision we have Jesus, who is for Judas, and on the other side we have Judas, who is against the one who is for him. "The New Testament gives us no direct information about the outcome of this extraordinary 'for and against.' Really none!"[67] Barth expanded on this dramatic claim by pointing out that "we actually know of only one certain triumph of hell—the handing-over of Jesus—and that this triumph of hell took place in order that it would never again be able to triumph."[68] We do not know if those who are (or seem to be) rejected in this life are in fact utterly lost. Judas therefore, poses a question that can only be left unanswered.

In making these claims, Barth clearly refused to abandon hope, even for Judas. At the same time, Barth puzzled over whether it is possible for those who are objectively saved and redeemed (because of the reality of what Christ has done for them) to persist in subjective denial of the real basis of their lives. It is natural to apply this question to Judas, who as far as we know lacked the faith that acknowledges and therefore receives God's gift of himself. If Judas did not say "I will" to the God who says "Call on Me," how can he be redeemed?

This question about the disjunct between our subjective experience of a fallen and broken world and Christian belief that in Christ we are made new is one we can hardly help posing, not just in Judas's case but in our own cases as well. After all, we all to one degree or another lack the signs of faith, hope, and love that are supposed to characterize life in Christ. But, in keeping with his views about assurance, Barth insisted that any appearance of conflict between the objective and subjective will be overcome and revealed to be a lie. Given who God is, it is inconceivable that false witness could have more permanence than true witness. The former has objectively been overcome by the death and resurrection of Christ.[69] It cannot really be the case that human beings will or even can choose to throw away God's mercy. For that possibility to be actual, God would have to be something other than who Barth believed God to be, as revealed in Christ.

At the same time, he refused to speculate about how or when Judas might have been or yet be saved. The most obvious possibility for salvation is that God might allow some kind of postmortem opportunity, a chance to cast himself on God's mercy even after death. That, however, is not a topic theologians can do anything more than speculate about, and Barth did not wish to speculate. Therefore, he restricted his discussion of Judas's fate to the contents of the biblical text. Barth was convinced that Christ's grace is irresistible, but he recognized that Judas is portrayed in the text as without hope, in the end. That is as much as we are told. And since God is not under any obligation to save or to damn, we are not in a position to make a doctrine according to which either of these outcomes is presumed.

It should be clear, however, that Barth's resistance to a doctrine of universalism did not mean that he considered universal salvation and limited salvation to be equal possibilities. The Christian has to hope and trust in the former, because to do otherwise would be to limit Christ. As a sign of hope in this possibility of redemption for Judas, Barth returned at the end of his excursus to the theme with which his reflections on Judas had begun. It is telling, he argued, that

The act of Judas cannot, therefore, be considered an unfortunate episode, much less as the manifestation of a dark realm beyond the will and work of God, but in every respect...as one element of the divine will and work. In what he himself wills and carries out, Judas does what God wills to be done.[70]

Barth's theological argument in the passage that surrounds this quote was more implicit than explicit, but the case he made is insightful. If God has drawn into his service even this one who by his own lights sought to abandon and betray his calling, then Judas cannot simply be said to have revolted against God. Nor can we easily say that he was despised or condemned by God, who acted under God's Lordship. This is why "[h]is election excels and outshines and controls and directs his rejection."[71] Barth's hope for even Judas's eventual salvation was based not just on a desire for God to be gracious, but in a sense of the fittingness of God redeeming those who have served God's purpose. Perhaps that purpose left them in an earthly or nonearthly hell of their own making for some time (again, Barth refused to speculate). Everyday experience suggests that in the short run God permits God's own powerful salvation to be ignored and violated in all sorts of ways. But whatever might or might not be permitted or determined along the way, Barth found it difficult to believe that the God revealed in Christ would permit a perverse "I will not" to be the end of the story.

Those who were handed over to wrath in scripture are, Barth argued, never mentioned without a direct or indirect reference to the eschatological possibility of a saving aim and meaning. Punishment is, therefore, always put into the service of redemption. Given this and the other aspects of Barth's doctrine of election we have discussed, it is clear that the whole logic of Barth's theology pushed him to hope for universal salvation. Without that hope his doctrine of predestination would have been as disturbing and unreassuring as he believed traditional doctrines of predestination had been. At the same time, he acknowledged that there is much we do not understand, and must wait to find out. A central theological challenge of his treatment of election was to keep these themes in the proper tension. "If we are certainly forbidden to count on this as though we had a claim to it...we are surely commanded the more definitely to hope and pray for it."[72] As in the relation between divine and human agency, the accent was particularly on one side. Christians are called to hope, not only in their own salvation, but for that of others, and thus to be "witnesses that God, like themselves, has not abandoned man and will not do so, that his kingdom, the kingdom of the Father, Son, and Holy Spirit, has come and will come even for him, that Jesus Christ is his hope too."[73]

6

Predestination: A moderate defense

In this concluding chapter, I offer a restrained defense of predestination. I do not claim that predestination is true, or that it is an essential part of Christian doctrine. However, I do suggest that belief in predestination is more reasonable, and less problematic, than is now widely believed. The doctrine of predestination has certainly been abused and misused in a variety of ways, but so have most influential ideas, over time. An idea this ancient and important has had more opportunities to be abused than most. But even if the doctrine has been problematic in multiple forms at various times, we may nevertheless be able to find forms of the doctrine worth affirming. We have seen that the doctrines of predestination articulated by its most prominent defenders are thoughtful and rich. This opens up the possibility of appropriating the best insights these traditional figures had to offer in order to propose a doctrine or doctrines of predestination we too could affirm. Here I attempt to defend only a minimal doctrine of predestination that draws insights from a number of the authors we have surveyed. My moderate defense of that doctrine will be that we can and should remain open to the possibility that predestination is true. This thesis might initially sound so weak as to be banal, but we will see that it has significant implications.

What, then, is the minimal doctrine of predestination that I mean to defend? I myself find supralapsarianism appealing, but the doctrine I have in mind is neutral on that question; it could go either way. In order to be a genuine doctrine of predestination, it must distinguish predestination from mere foreknowledge, and thus part ways with Anselm's approach. Here I follow Aquinas's definition of predestination as God's "ordering of some persons towards eternal salvation," a decree that exists first in God's mind and is then enacted in history.[1] The doctrine I defend is "hopeful," in that it shares Augustine's understanding of predestination as an order of grace. Whether it should be called a doctrine of double or single predestination is not a question I address, as I have questions about how helpful those terms are. I am more interested in how predestination relates to the possibilities of universal salvation or the reprobation of some, a question I leave open for now. Either possibility can be added to the minimal doctrine of predestination I defend, and both will be considered below. My minimal doctrine departs from Luther and Calvin by clearly distinguishing predestination from divine determinism. Predestination implies divine determination of at least some very important aspects of creaturely life, namely whether those creatures are ordered to everlasting union with God. Being ordered toward eternal salvation does not, however, require complete determinism. God could very well permit multiple paths to a particular end, or determine some crucial matters while leaving matters of less significance indeterministic. It may also be that determinism of some sort or other—modern mechanistic conceptions of determinism are not the only possibility—does apply. It makes sense for a minimal doctrine of predestination to be agnostic about such matters, however.

I am going to take for granted that this minimal doctrine of predestination receives support from the Bible as well as from prominent Christian theologians. This is not to deny that there may be other intelligent ways to read some of these traditions, especially the biblical indications. My assumption is simply that on fairly plain readings, it looks rather like there are significant predestinarian themes in the Bible and other parts of the Christian theological tradition. These themes are generally avoided, rejected, or reinterpreted not because it is unreasonable to interpret them as supporting doctrines of predestination but because many theists would prefer not to believe in predestination. Their reservations about predestination are not mainly textual but conceptual, oriented (as I have been assuming throughout this book) around one or both of two closely connected concerns. These are, first, that doctrines of predestination lead to problematic conceptions of human agency, or of the relationship between divine and human agency, and second, that doctrines of predestination undermine attempts to deal with the problem of evil. The case I make for predestination in this chapter focuses on those two concerns, on the supposition that if these concerns can be addressed predestination should, at the very least, not be ruled out. For theists who embrace the *prima facie* support for predestination provided by the Augustinian tradition and biblical indications, it may, in fact, be ruled in.

1. Hope in predestination

I argue below that a moderate defender of predestination can defuse the attacks most often pressed against it. The doctrine need not be fatalistic or callous. However, it seems appropriate to begin a defense of predestination by making a positive case for the doctrine. Even if there are not good reasons to disbelieve the doctrine, we would like to know whether there are positive reasons to believe in it. Here I offer two. The first is that because of the assurance offered by the idea that God predestines, we have reason to hope that predestination is true. The second is that because they help us grapple with the role of luck and powerlessness in our lives, doctrines of predestination lay open significant insights into the human condition.

The virtue for which the doctrine of predestination is best known is its assurance—all will be well. This affirmation expresses not merely a trust in divine sovereignty, as is often said, but more deeply a hopefulness about the sovereign God's intentions toward us and the whole of creation. In spite of the deeply confusing, often contradictory, sometimes beautiful and sometimes tragic events we see in the world around us, we may trust that the story of the world is ultimately one of joy (in the old sense of the word, a comedy) and not tragedy. This is a powerful source of hope.

Predestination most obviously offers hope on approaches like Barth's, which either decisively or hopefully affirm universal salvation as the logic of Christian faith. Such views need not be complacent about evil or take sin lightly. They are not blindly optimistic. They grant that this life has many trials, and allow for the possibility that God punishes in ways that fall short of being eternal. They recognize that heavenly life itself may contain difficult lessons that require growth. They affirm, however, that God elects all of humanity to participate in the overcoming of sin and evil that marks history's final and decisive trajectory.

Those who believe in hell must necessarily temper such claims. Yet nonuniversalistic doctrines of predestination can provide a similar sense of hope, and go a long way toward avoiding traditional problems of assurance, to the degree that they emphasize (1) the "wideness" of God's mercy, and (2) the necessity of trusting divine grace alone for confidence about eternal destinies. They become problematic to the degree that they encourage those who want to hope to instead question divine intentions and to look to themselves for signs of their ultimate destiny. Even at their best, views on which some human beings are reprobate raise questions about divine goodness that universalist views do not (see section 5). Nevertheless, they can be a significant source of assurance.

By contrast, a libertarian picture of the world, where individuals make their meaning on their own terms and by their own lights, undermines the hope that a divine power orders all things toward meaning rather than chaos. Libertarianism constrains divine meaning-making because libertarian freedom would be impaired if the deep significance of our choices were being maneuvered by God in ways unknown to us. That would imply that we were not really in charge of the significance of our stories. The hope in doctrines of predestination, however, is precisely of this sort. It is a trust that our small and fumbling contributions can be and indeed are being woven into something much greater than ourselves.

Predestination is hopeful not only on a large scale but in terms of personal narratives as well. A widely shared fear is the concern that our lives may amount to nothing, that we have been on the wrong path but do not know it, that our time has been wasted. To be sure, the hope that God predestines does not imply that every event in our lives is for the best, or has rich hidden meaning. It does not assure us that we have made no genuine mistakes or that particular encounters with evil are for the best. This is perhaps most obvious if the world is generally indeterministic, since all predestination means in such a case is that ultimate things will turn out well. As Luther theorized, it is possible within such a framework that lesser things are permitted to go various ways. Even so, it is deeply meaningful to be able to hope that one's wanderings and sufferings are ultimately under a guiding hand wiser and stronger than one's own. This hope implies that life's troubles may very well be redeemed, and brought to mean something positive. At the least, one may hope that evil will be defeated, unable to overcome positive meaning and beauty in one's existence. Such hopes are of great value, enough to keep one from despair and to motivate continued efforts to seek, promote, and enjoy the good.

The hope that doctrines of predestination offer can and for many believers already does motivate belief in predestination. Yet the hope that creatures are destined for ultimate good does not count as evidence for predestination, at least on traditional conceptions of evidence. Hope can nevertheless count as a positive reason for embracing the idea that God predestines. As I understand it, hoping in the sort of predestination sketched above does not require one to have a high level of conviction about the truth of predestination. One may remain open to the possibility that predestination is false while hoping that it is true, because of the inspiring qualities of the doctrine. Robert Pasnau's characterization of hope as opposed to fear is helpful here.[2] Those who hope may not be sure how to adjudicate the likelihood of the object of their hope, but part of what it means to hope is to attend more to the possibility of success than failure. This is why hope plays the role it does in motivating us. Hope, especially an ultimate hope such as the hope that God destines the story of our world to turn out well and better than well, enables us to persist in the face of discouragement; it makes us resilient.

Having hope requires a conviction that the object of hope is not impossible, and that what is hoped for is not irrational. So hope is not disconnected from belief, or from the wider contents of one's faith. It seems appropriate to say that one who hopes in predestination has at least a weak belief in it. Hope, after all, is both an affective and a cognitive virtue. In its expectancy it does not ignore available evidence but it rightly does not simply make bets according to what appear to be the probabilities. Rather, it courageously holds on to its expectation, even against the odds. Those who regard hope as a virtue should endorse the rationality and propriety of doing so. On this analysis, then, it makes sense for theists who believe that God is love to hope that God predestines. Surely the theist may hope that God rules over all things in order to bring them to a conclusion that displays the goodness of the divine plan from the beginning. Indeed, as Barth argued, such a hope seems fitting for those who believe that God is revealed in Jesus Christ, in whose life even death serves a greater victory.

2. Predestination, luck, and control

Trust in predestination is a source of hope in another way—it makes it easier to accept realities of human agency that are otherwise hard to face. Paradoxically, it does so by highlighting ways in which our lives are, at least from a penultimate perspective, often unfair, out of our control, and at the mercy of luck. As we have seen, doctrines of predestination imply that basic facts about human identities and destinies are out of our control. They therefore imply that all of us are affected in deep ways by something akin to what Thomas Nagel has called constitutive luck—luck in the makeup of our core identities.[3] Given this connection, is it not surprising that doctrines of predestination have typically been correlated with theologies of sin and grace that emphasize the limits of human agency. Highlighting these aspects of human agency has not always made predestinarian soteriologies well liked, but they are not unique in indicating that significant aspects of our lives are out of our control. What is unique about them is their claim that this lack of control may be something for which we can be grateful, and which makes us better off than we would be if the meaning of our stories were up to us. If the ultimate story of the world is one in which love precedes merit, luck matters less than we might have thought. Not everything depends on things being fair, because the point of creation is not merely just deserts.

For many of us, however, it is natural to believe that the meaning of our lives ought to be something we have earned, and that it is only fair for the significance of our lives to be something that we have chosen. This requires us to be the sources of our stories. Thus, we tend to celebrate not stoic resignation but self-made men who turned their lives around or beat the odds. We find it frustrating when we lack control, and we often distance ourselves from aspects of our stories that we have not intentionally authored. That is one reason why doctrines of predestination are uncomfortable for us. Predestination, after all, suggests that significant aspects of our stories have been written in advance, by a hand other than our own. How, we wonder, can our stories be fair and meaningful if we are not in charge of their direction?

Defenders of predestination sometimes attempt to answer these questions by appealing to mystery or paradox. We have seen, however, that they can do better, with the help of a noncompetitive approach to divine and human agency, cashed out in terms of the sort of compatibilism we have seen Augustine, Aquinas, Calvin, and even to some degree Luther defend. Their Augustinian compatibilism helps us see how we can be meaningful, responsible, and free agents in the context of divine rule. We can summarize the shared elements of Augustinian compatibilism metaphorically, with the suggestion that if God elects to make us conversation partners who speak with our own distinctive voices, we play an important role in history. To paraphrase Luther, history is decided not simply by us, but not without us. Thus, Augustinian compatibilists would note, it is not quite right to say that if predestination is true, our histories are written by a hand other than our own. God predestines human beings to be personal agents who also write too, hand in hand with God. Humanity is elected and created to play an essential role in the direction of history. Given the sort of creatures we have been made to be, we act responsively and in a broad sense rationally. We are motivated, for instance, by our loves and our ideals, by a desire to avoid punishment, and by the feelings we have when we are blamed or praised. What happens in history thus takes place because of our beliefs, our desires, and our actions. That gives us a deep ownership of that history. We are not merely mechanical causes; we are personally responsible agents. So on a compatibilist account, human beings can be quite momentous actors in the world. What we do, and what we want to do, matters even in cases where God has ordained that things could not be otherwise. Indeed, our personal agency often shines forth the most in the cases where we have just one way forward because the path is illuminated for us by our loves. In such cases, doing anything else is not forced but it is, practically speaking, unthinkable (a point any coffee lover understands when presented with a perfect cappuccino).

An updated Augustinian compatibilism can develop the intuitive claims made above with the suggestion that human beings are personally responsible not most fundamentally for what they control, but for what they own (in a deep sense of that term). What they own is what reflects on them as persons—their beliefs and desires, and the actions or inactions motivated by them.[4] As Calvin pointed out, responsible agency is undermined by being forced to act, but we can distinguish between being determined and being forced. God's gracious agency is such that it does not force. Rather, God is able to direct our paths by directly and indirectly shaping human beliefs and desires. Divine determinations thus shape us at the most basic level, the level of who we are. On this view, human persons are both active and passive. We are passive in that we do not make ourselves. Yet we are also active in our attitudes and emotions, which make us the personal agents we are. Augustinian compatibilists should agree that ownership without control may not create high levels of responsibility; if we had libertarian free will we might very well be accountable for more. The Augustinian claims, however, that even agents who lack control can have an important kind of personal agency, to which we rightly respond by offering credit and censure. What matters about our agency is not simply our choices. Our attitudes and emotions are morally and spiritually significant in their own right.

Even so briefly characterized, Augustinian compatibilism offers a glimpse of why it makes sense to claim that divine determination is compatible with free and responsible human agency. At the same time, it is important to note that Augustinian compatibilism does not require one to believe in the actuality of divine determination of any sort, including predestination. It might turn out to be the case that some sort of indeterminism is actually the way of things, and if so, the compatibilist account of personal agency just sketched would not be thrown into confusion.

Describing Augustinian compatibilism as a noncompetitive view of the relation between divine and human action is appropriate but also incomplete, because (as we have seen) that phrase can mean many things. Defenders of predestination should grant that if we do not have the option of making history turn out other than God has already elected, that makes human agency much less powerful, at least in certain respects, than libertarian intuitions presume. Openness to the possibility that God predestines requires giving up an idea of human autonomy that many cherish. Accordingly, the sort of divine and human agency that are, on a predestinarian view, noncompetitive cannot just be of any sort. Rather, a particular conception of both is required.

At the same time, less is lost in giving up a libertarian picture of human agency than we might think. After all, if the idea that we make our own meaning does not actually fit our reality, it is better to give up on it. Refusing to do so has the unfortunate consequence of asking of human agency more than it can bear. Indeed, from the perspective of predestination it would actually be gracious for God not to put too much into our hands, given our limited capacities. Let me now develop these claims further.

It is, I have noted, a common experience that the meaning of our lives is in significant respects not within our grasp. Deep aspects of our identities, including many of our talents and interests, are given to us at birth or aroused in us by the circumstances in which we grew up. Whether such deep facts about our constitutions should in fact be called *luck* is unclear—luck would seem to apply to existing beings, for which things could have gone better or worse. It does not make much sense to say that I am lucky to have been appointed by God to be human, or to live in this modern age rather than one in which I would not have had access to reading glasses. I am grateful for these gifts but it is doubtful that *I* could be very much otherwise and remain myself. It may be better, therefore, not to use the metaphor of a birth lottery but simply to consider the lack of control we have over the deep aspects of our identities we owe to the spiritual, genetic, and environmental powers that make us. The idea of predestination is both unsettling and compelling because it points so clearly to this theme, our notable lack of control.

Our lack of control extends to factors that can clearly be called luck. Situational luck in the good or bad options we face (some are forced to choose between saving their families and standing up to oppression), and outcome luck in how the things we attempt turn out and are received by others (some drunk drivers hit no one, some beautiful works of art never find their audience) are constant features of our lives. They often combine. We can, for instance, exercise our powers to their fullest and fail to get a good job (or a job at all!) if the timing is wrong. As sports statisticians have shown with particular clarity, good performances are often overlooked by managers whose ideas about success may be based on superficialities. Success in our personal relationships, too, has a sobering amount to do with being in the right place in the right time, not to mention the vagaries of the goodwill of others. In all these ways, luck plays a huge role in how things turn out for us. It is our everyday experience that the meanings of significant aspects of our lives are deeply vulnerable to the influence of powers beyond our control, for ill and for good.

Moral luck (luck that affects a person's moral capacities, accomplishments, and standing) offers a particularly powerful and poignant example of this point. Luther is hardly alone in his having found that his day-to-day choices did not necessarily add up to the ability to choose the most noteworthy features of his own character. He wanted to eradicate fear and pride in his attitudes, but found a vicious circularity in that the more he tried to attend to his own character the more his problems of fear and pride grew. Hence, his mistrust of Aristotle's idea that we can create virtuous habits in ourselves through the repetition of good actions. His failure to build a more virtuous Luther from the bottom-up surely helped to convince him that our personalities require revolutionary rather than incremental change if real growth is to occur. Most of us are more inclined than Luther to believe in the possibility of building virtuous habits by practicing good action, but he was surely on to an important truth about our moral lives. We all have experience with the gaps and mysteries that beset our best attempts at moral improvement. Sometimes good intentions and clever strategies for moral formation seem to help us improve ourselves (or others), but other times, not.

In some respects, we are in an even better position than Luther to see the significant ways in which moral accomplishment and standing depend on factors beyond our control. Research in the behavioral sciences that now spans decades has only fueled the claim that we have less control over the shape our stories take than we are inclined to believe. We have found that our stories happen to us at least as much as we make them happen. This is not surprising once we realize that although we are deeply rational beings much of our behavior is guided by unconscious intuitions and heuristics. Moreover, our beliefs and cares are systematically shaped by genetic, environmental, and interpersonal influences in ways we only sometimes understand.

One compelling example of these points can be found in the psychological literature exploring the influence situational factors have on human behavior. This research suggests that what character we have tends to be weak and rather easily influenced. For instance, studies on cheating consistently show that a great many people cheat, when they think they can get away with it. But cheating behavior can be manipulated to become more serious or more common if subjects hope to avoid some anticipated discomfort to themselves. It can also be manipulated to become significantly more rare by reminding study participants of the immorality of cheating ahead of time. This seems to suggest that the cheating impulse is typically mixed with a desire to see oneself as honest, and that which motive "wins" has a good deal to do with the luck of which environmental cues become salient to us at a given time.[5] Similar lessons can be drawn from studies on the way in which generosity can be manipulated by exposing subjects to a small positive event (such as finding a coin) just before they are given an opportunity to help.[6] The upshot of these and many related studies is that most of us are volitionally and cognitively fractured enough that our moral and immoral behaviors are rather easily swayed, often by factors of which we are not fully aware.

Ironically, at the same time that research on the situational influences on behavior has undermined the notion of agential autonomy, ongoing research on the "illusion of control" has found that we have a chronic tendency to assume we have control in cases where we do not, and to assume that we have more control than we actually do in cases where we do. This has been shown even with simple actions like picking lottery tickets or rolling the dice—certifiably random activities that many research subjects nevertheless believed they could influence via their carefully selected choices and actions.[7] It is plausible, according to this research, that we tend to impute control to ourselves when we intend things to happen, and they do. Often, however, especially in complex situations such as succeeding in a career, in parenting, or in a friendship, the connection between intending an outcome and making it happen is far from clear. And even when we do succeed in directing our lives in the way we want them to go, we often find that our accomplishments do not mean what we expected. Luther may be an example here again, given the way his attempts to reform the church led unexpectedly to schism instead. This point echoes a great theme of Augustine's *Confessions*, which is that the meaning and significance of our lives is obscure to us, and thus in significant ways not up to us.

So much sober realism about the limits of our control could lead to nihilism or feelings of helplessness. It is perhaps not accidental that psychologists who study the illusion of control have found a correlation between higher levels of realism about control and depression. However, as Augustine realized long ago, doctrines of predestination reorient rather than undermine our sense of meaning and accomplishment in life. Pagan doctrines of the meaninglessness of the universe and the accidental quality of the life in it do seem to lead toward despair. Those, however, are doctrines of an absolute lack of direction in the universe. Predestination, by contrast, is a doctrine that implies a relative lack of control on our parts, but also a much more fundamental context of divine control, in which our own efforts, feeble and fragmentary as they may be, participate in and contribute to something much greater.

Naturally, these ideas raise questions about the extent to which those whom God predestines should be said to deserve credit (or blame) for whatever virtue (or vice) they may have. We have seen Calvin and others suggest that one implication of a doctrine of predestination is that the elect cannot claim credit for whatever virtues they may have, because the good in our lives is a gift. The truth in this approach is their reminder that salvation is not based on human merit, because grace is prevenient. It seems inconsistent, however, to blame those whose vices are not simply up to them but not to give any credit to saints whose virtue is not simply up to them. It is better to nuance the sense in which both credit and blame apply if predestination is true. My suggestion is that both apply in a limited but real way, such that to whatever extent a person's virtues or vices are predestined (and, again, on a minimal account of predestination it is possible that this is quite a complex matter) that person should be said to have responsibility not for having come to have them, but simply for having them. St. Paul's zeal for the gospel, to take one of Augustine's favored examples, is not something he gained for himself. It was a gift of operative grace. He did, however, have that zeal, in that it was his own belief in Christ and desire to share with others that gave rise to the zeal he had. He can, therefore, be praised for it, though not in as many ways or to as great a degree as he would were it simply his choice. We should also add that his responsibility for his missional character was clearly shared with the God who had turned his life around. Thus, he should give credit where it is due even while he is praised.

Correspondingly, it may well be that Judas's falsehood as a friend was also predestined, which according to Augustinian compatibilism implies that he is less blameworthy than we might otherwise think. He remains blameworthy, because it is bad to have the sort of evil will required to betray a friend. Still, we should blame Judas less than we would if he had more control over his destiny. This attenuation of blame is not just because of his limited agency, though that is an important part of it. We would, to offer an analogy, feel bad for a betrayer of friends who had been raised not to trust or depend on anyone, perhaps by cruel parents, even though we would presumably also blame that child once grown into a man whose cynical view of the world was that all relationships are limited engagements of self-interest. It is interesting that for all we know Judas had such a back-story. It is telling that we do not reserve judgment of him on this account—to some degree certain details of his personal history make no difference to us. He was, after all, a bad man. Yet for all that, as the doctrine of predestination points out, his character formation was in certain respects in the hands of others. If he was constituted a betrayer, that does seem to dilute his personal responsibility. If he was elected to betray, we may pity him for that, as well as blame him. And here Judas may represent many sinners, whose vices and evil deeds are (to varying extents) not simply the product of their self-conscious choices but the accidental byproducts of their own lack of foresight or their formation by others.

The doctrine of predestination also raises a further question, not so much concerning Judas's degree of personal responsibility as the extent to which he can be blamed for his betrayal. If, as Barth argued, Judas was in a way serving God, should he be praised, or at least blamed less? Perhaps in some respects it was lucky for him that his betrayal led to a great good. That may in a limited respect make it less bad, without simply making it good. To say this is, of course, to fully embrace the idea of moral luck, but also to suggest that in some cases luck may have little to do with it.

The idea of predestination pushes us to ask deep questions we otherwise tend to ignore, not only concerning how much control we have, but how much control we should desire. What initially seems distressing can come to seem a blessing as we ponder whether it may, in fact, be our good luck that human existence is not simply fair but is instead ordered toward grace. It is doubtful that we should really want to be fully in charge of our lives, given how little we know and how short-sighted our aspirations and plans tend to be. Thus, if doctrines of predestination teach that we have less autonomy than we like to think, they are nevertheless hopeful in reframing our lack of power as in actuality not much of a loss. Those who emphasize the prevenience of divine grace acknowledge that it is better to be part of God's story than an independent author. This too fits our experience, since much of what is best in our lives, after all, is not what we have chosen but what we have been given. These things include our families, our counties, and many of the other things we love as well, goods which we discover as part of who we are rather than choose.

A doctrine of predestination is no guarantee that one's everyday life is well lived—even if Judas is ultimately destined for glory, his life is forever marked by his betrayal of a friend. Yet on a wider perspective, doctrines of predestination offer a serenity about ultimate things that can give us respite from the fear of failure and the paralysis such fear can bring. If we are sole authors of our stories, it would make sense to be fraught with worry over whether we have written well. By contrast, if God predestines, we need not worry about being the ultimate arbiters of the meaning of our lives. Accepting the lack of control we have over so many aspects of life, we may trust that we are ruled by the loving hand of a personal God, not fumbling beneath the indifferent forces of chance or fate. And we may hope that as secondary coauthors we are participating in writing stories more rich and profound than we would tell on our own.

3. A problem of libertarian assurance

I have argued that doctrines of predestination can be a significant source of hope. This hope is not blind. Indeed, it may enable us to grapple with aspects of the human condition from which we are otherwise prone to avert our eyes. Predestination will remain hard to accept, however, for those who remain committed to a libertarian view of human freedom or responsibility. Therefore, in sections 3 and 4 of this chapter, building on the points about luck and lack of control made in section 2, I offer two arguments that weigh against libertarianism.

These arguments draw on Luther and Barth's concerns about theological speculation. Readers of previous chapters will note that I criticized both authors for their implementation of this concern. In my view, theologians should not seek to do without philosophy, both because this allows philosophical ideas to surreptitiously influence theology and because a lack of philosophical development so easily undermines the task of theology, which is to give an account of our faith and hope. Developing a philosophical account that fits and informs the theological beliefs one has is an essential way for faith to seek understanding.

Luther and Barth were nevertheless right to be concerned about speculation. In the light of this general concern about conjecture, I offer two indirect arguments that favor predestination. In keeping with my moderate approach, these are not arguments for the truth of predestination but rather arguments against the libertarian views that rule predestination out because it is a divine determination. My assumption is that if libertarianism is seen to be weak, we are left with two options. We can give up on free will and responsible agency or, preferably, we can accept a compatibilist account. Accepting a theologically informed compatibilism does not necessarily mean accepting predestination, but it does leave that possibility open.

Let us begin by reminding ourselves that libertarian views like Anselm's require human agents to be the ultimate sources of their own actions and attitudes, and to accomplish that feat by way of their own undetermined choices. My contention is that such views have a problem of assurance. Libertarians reject predestination because it violates their conception of free agency, but in doing so they take an undue risk. This risk is generated by the fact that predestination cannot be ruled out. Even if one's favored theory of free will or approach to theodicy gives one reason to disfavor predestination, it may very well be the case that God predestines. This possibility should particularly be taken seriously by those who hold anything like traditional theistic beliefs in an all-powerful and omniscient God whose promises can be trusted and whose knowledge is sure. If such a God exists, divine determinations of various sorts may also exist, predestination among them.[8]

The mere fact that an idea cannot be ruled out is not by itself a good reason to remain open to it, of course. We cannot rule out the possibility that the world will end tomorrow but it is unreasonable to let that possibility have much influence on our planning. The difference in this case is the fact that we have a robust and independently plausible alternative to the libertarian views that cannot accept predestination, namely some variation on the noncompetitive compatibilist views discussed throughout this book.

Compatibilist views have the significant comparative advantage that they do not put us in a position of needing to radically revise our views about human agency if some day we find out that predestination is in fact true. Predestination may be true or may be false, but an Augustinian or other compatibilist can accept this uncertainty, and is in a strong position either way. Whether predestination is true or not, compatibilists can affirm that human beings are genuine dialogue partners with God, who God rightly treats with the full status of persons. Either way, we are responsible agents whose freedom is not in competition with divine determination. Because compatibilism is open to a variety of ways of thinking about creation, providence, and so on, it is quite flexible.[9] It does not place weighty demands on a person's theological convictions but allows those convictions to be developed in thoughtful ways.

By contrast, libertarianism is far more intrusive. It places substantial limits on what a person of faith may confess. Moreover, because libertarians suppose that we are only responsible for undetermined choices, they entangle theologians in unnecessary speculation about the nature of the world and of the divine economy. Libertarians must bet that predestination is false, in spite of the difficulty of adjudicating the extremely complex questions raised by doctrines of predestination (not to mention associated doctrines of divine foreknowledge, grace, and sin). If it were to be discovered that predestination were in fact true, they would be thrown into disarray. Counterintuitively, it would turn out that human beings are not free or responsible agents, and that divine grace undermines rather than uplifts us. The unappealing nature of this possibility counts against libertarianism. It is widely taken for granted that most everyday human beings are responsible and accountable agents who are worthy of at least some degree of praise and blame—and this conviction is worth holding on to. It is a point in favor of compatibilist accounts that they make it possible to hold onto that conviction in a far wider range of cases than do libertarian accounts.

4. The scarcity of libertarian freedom

The observation that compatibilism is less speculative than libertarianism counts in favor of predestination, because it gives us a reason to hold a theory of agency that does not put predestination at odds with freedom or responsibility. A second indirect consideration that favors predestination is the fact that libertarian free choice appears to be extremely rare, if it exists at all. This is another kind of problem of libertarian assurance, which I will call the problem of scarcity. The problem is generated by the extremely high bar set for free and responsible agency on libertarian theories, which call for a power analogous to God's ability to be an ultimate source of action, not determined by any other. The difficulty is, again, that our world, our relationship with God, or our natures may not fit those requirements. Agency has to work in a very particular manner in order for persons to independently control their own fates. Thus, even if we sometimes have libertarian free choices, it seems unlikely that we have them often enough to justify our common practices of praise, blame, punishment, and so on. Rather than abandon those practices, it is better to accept a less-demanding theory of agency.

In order to inquire further into the scarcity problem, it is important to clarify what it means to have a "significant" free choice, and why that matters to libertarians. In our discussion of Luther in Chapter Four a significant choice was simply one that made a moral or spiritual difference. For libertarians, by contrast, whether a choice is significant matters because only significant choices are self-defining in the ways libertarians believe they need to be in order to ground free will and moral responsibility. Consider the following example: on a whim I decide to take the long route when driving some friends home. Unbeknownst to me, this saves our lives because I fail to drive over a bridge that would have collapsed as we crossed. In this instance, the ramifications of my choice far exceed what I can be credited for. I saved our lives, but that was merely a fortunate accident. For a choice to be significant in the libertarian sense it therefore has to be under my control by being voluntary, self-aware, and intentional.

Libertarian free choices must also be undetermined, but a corollary of the point that libertarian choices must be significant is the fact that mere indeterminism is not enough for libertarian agency. The results of my choices cannot simply be accidental if they are to be my way of your writing my own story. Our question, then, is not simply whether human beings have choices but whether we very often have choices that are significant in the ways just described.[10]

Clearly, if some sort of physical or divine determinism is true, significant libertarian choices do not exist at all—that, as we have seen, is a source of uncertainty for the libertarian view that the compatibilist can largely shrug off. However, even putting questions about the reality of determinism to one side, we may ask how common significant choices are, given what we think we know about the world.

One reason to believe that significant libertarian free choices are scarce is the fact (related to the question of constitutional luck discussed above) that our choices are typically motivated by beliefs and cares that we did not choose to have but rather find ourselves with. That our choices are motivated should not be controversial. Even when we are not aware of our motives others are often able to see what motivates us. Even when we act oddly or arbitrarily we have our reasons. Moreover, such motivations need not operate deterministically. Perhaps the beliefs that are salient to us at any given time are somewhat random. The point is simply that if our choices were not motivated by our reasons and desires they would not be rational or explicable, and it would be difficult even to attribute them to us.

The difficulty for the libertarian is that the beliefs and cares that motivate our choices do not themselves generally appear to be the products of our significant choices. Even important decisions such as whether to attend college, what to major in, whether to marry, and so on, are deeply shaped by environmental cues and social currents that we have not chosen and that we often fail to comprehend. Our decisions about these topics find their source in conceptions of self and the good life over which we have, at best, limited volitional control. How then can we achieve independent self-determination? Mere indeterminism regarding which competing motivational factor wins out does not give us the kind of control over our identities that libertarians require. The puzzle, then, is how it is possible to regularly have the kind of self-determining power that libertarians prize.

This problem is made more difficult by the fact that libertarian choice is an achievement of a higher degree of conscious agency than is typical for human beings. Average agents are not especially self-reflective. For the most part, most of us, most of the time, are disinclined to think hard or long about our fundamental values, ends, and commitments. To some degree this is because doing so is somewhat frightening, and psychologically taxing in other ways as well. We are also rather busy, with many obligations to fulfill, and often have little time to reflect. Moreover, quite often we simply do not realize what our values and motivations are. Because we see the world through them, they are opaque to us. It can require considerable insight, mentoring, and effort for a person to be able to see that she or he could have different interests or commitments.

Typically, we act on the basis of notions and interests that we picked up at one time or another without having struggled too much over whether to appropriate them. Even many of the important turning points in our lives are unaccompanied by conscious choices. We often fail to realize the import of an event until we look back, at which point we realize that a particular conversation or experience mattered deeply. At other times we know something important is happening to us, but we have little control over it. Perhaps we meet someone and "fall for them," have an experience of God's immediacy in a religious service, or see something in a movie that touches us. Such turning points are not a product of conscious choice even though they are reorienting in important ways. Indeed, one of the mistakes libertarianism incentivizes is the idea that these experiences are less important aspects of our personal identities than our undetermined, conscious choices. If anything, things are often the other way around.

The scarcity problem, then, is created by the difficulty of navigating between two poles. For a decision to be more than the mere result of chance it must be a choice that can be explained in terms of the agents' existing personality and convictions, but if the choice can be explained by such factors it becomes difficult to see why we should also say that it is independently sourced in an undetermined (and somewhat mysterious) power of libertarian free will. It is difficult to tell whether any of our choices avoid this libertarian Scylla and Charybdis, and unlikely that many do. This places libertarians in an uncomfortable position, because they ask us to relate to one another as if we had libertarian free choice, and are subject to the high agential demands that go with it, even though they can only speculate that we do in fact have such power to shape ourselves.

Another aspect of the scarcity problem, already touched on, concerns the worrisome implications of prioritizing conscious choice as the central feature of human agency. Doing so unduly shrinks the sphere of responsible and free agency, and shifts our attention away from core elements of human experience.

Consider the following tale: a person of average intellectual and other abilities is born with typical predispositions to trust and learn, raised in an evangelical household, goes to Church, Christian schools, and so on, and happily lives out of the values she has been taught. By the age of 21, she has not faced a situation that has led her to reevaluate her fundamental commitments. She has never had a crisis of faith, and she has made no significant conscious choices concerning the ends she finds natural to follow. Her focus has been on choosing how to follow these ends, and trying to live up to her aspirations. Some will find her life colorless, but it is unlikely that we would treat her as if she is not morally responsible for her values or her actions. She may be responsible to a lesser degree than those who have carefully examined their commitments and reassessed them. At the very least, however, it seems clear that her lack of self-orienting choices does not mean that we cannot assess her for the convictions she lives out. If it did, the implications would be distressing, since it seems likely that much of humanity over the centuries has lived lives similar to that of this hypothetical evangelical.

Unfortunately, libertarians often argue that such persons are not morally responsible—for instance, some have suggested that unreflective Hitler Youth who were not presented with a choice about their beliefs were not blameworthy for their hatred of Jews.[11] This does not strike me as plausible. After all, we regularly blame (and sometimes punish) racists and sexists for their beliefs, actions, and emotions, regardless of whether they self-consciously chose to be that way—a fact we rarely can determine, and do not always even attempt to determine. We may hold that the responsibility of those who do not choose these things is less than those who do, but we still do hold them responsible. Any who sympathize with that approach must ask whether choice is as central to the moral life as libertarians typically maintain.

The libertarian emphasis on conscious and voluntary choices has the effect of divesting us of responsibility in a disturbingly large number of cases. For instance, omissions (such as not remembering your wedding anniversary, or simply failing to notice that a friend is "not himself") seem generally unintentional and even involuntary, but surely we are often responsible for them. Dispensing the wrong medicine to a patient or forgetting an important date *could* be the result of a previous intentional action, if you tried to make the mistake in question, or deliberately avoided doing something you knew would avoid the problem. Unfortunately, however, we often make such mistakes without having even considered the possibility that we might, and even if our character is not especially or intentionally bad in a relevant respect—so surely we cannot connect those mistakes to previous intentional actions. Yet it seems obvious that we are often responsible for such omissions and actions, and in fact we hold one another responsible for them regularly. All this suggests that making intentional, voluntary choices central to our conception of human agency limits our understanding of human agency in ways that are suspect.

Any theory of agency deals, at least implicitly, with the following question: who is the subject of our stories? In a theological context, libertarianism is powerful because of the fear that divine determination would erase us as agents, making us mere automatons, simple outworkings of another. The self-defining power of free choice offers a solution because it allows agents to take ownership of their stories and thus to receive credit or blame for them. A compatibilist take on the idea of predestination, by contrast, suggests that we have deep ownership of aspects of ourselves we do not control. It admits that control can be a good, but denies that it necessarily matters more to us (or to our practices of praise and blame) than other kinds of ownership. The contrast between these views highlights the fact that libertarianism depends on a controversial aspiration for moral agents, what we might call the "self-made self."[12] Self-made selves are special agents who are not essentially characterized by the sundry beliefs, values, and ends with which they find themselves; they rise above what is given about them to become autonomous. What they are accountable for is not being the persons they are, but more narrowly the story they tell via their choices. The implication is that their unchosen histories and relationships do not fundamentally constitute them; these factors are resources on which they draw.

Augustinians, like most compatibilists, favor a less metaphysically ambitious and individualistic view of the responsible self. Without denying the import of recognizing and developing the human capacity for reflective self-control, they note that what we care about and react to in others and ourselves encompasses a much wider agential circle. Reflective self-control may be a power of human action *par excellence*, but human action *par excellence* is not all there is to our morally and spiritually significant agency. Indeed, reflective self-control may not even be required for the best kind of human action. A less stereotypically Kantian and more Aristotelian picture of our moral and spiritual lives would suggest that human action *par excellence* is displayed by virtuous persons who do not struggle to control their ends or desires, and who do not need to weigh their options but who know the good and pursue it whole-heartedly. Especially when we have goodness of that sort, it is no terrible thing when we cannot separate ourselves from what we are given to be. That was one of the things Augustine and Aquinas were getting at when they suggested that Christ's human nature, which had no choice but to be good, is particularly free.

In conclusion, once we develop the implications of libertar-ianism, it appears to make us responsible for too little, because it requires from us a kind of agency that we rarely if ever achieve. Compatibilist views, by contrast, are more at home in the world in which we appear to live, and more at home with the nature of the agency we actually appear to have. Given these considerations, my preference is to leave open the possibility that we do at times have significant libertarian choices, but not to make much depend on that possibility. It is hard to tell how common such choices are, and an Augustinian compatibilist need not rule them out. At the same time, we have little evidence for their existence, and reason to think that they are not central to human agency.

5. Election, evil, and hell

I have argued that compatibilism should be a more attractive option for theists than libertarianism. Because it avoids undue speculation while developing the central theological claim that divine and human agency are not in competition, compatibilism makes it much easier to affirm a number of core traditional Christian doctrines, including the claim that God predestines.[13] It does not, however, address all the problems associated with predestination. In fact, the most difficult problem for doctrines of predestination may not be the questions about agency they raise but the questions they pose about God's relationship to evil. Even if predestined agents have genuine personal responsibility, what does it say about God if creatures are destined for evils such as sin or suffering, not to mention hell?

The problem of a predestining God's relation to evil can be ameliorated to some degree by appealing to the distinction between predestination and complete determinism. The problem of divine goodness is somewhat easier to handle if God does not directly ordain evil actions but rather permits them. The history of responses to Luther and Calvin's divine determinism suggests that it is easier to justify mere divine permission of creaturely evil. Divine determinism appears to mean that God actively ensures the existence of particular evils, raising the question of divine evil intent Calvin sought to address. By contrast, it is somewhat easier to distance God from evil if God's relationship to evil is indirect. The conclusion we should draw from this brief comparison is not simply that divine determinism should be rejected; it may be possible for theists to deal with the problems just mentioned.[14] However, because of the complexity of the territory a moderate defense of predestination can make its task somewhat easier by not defending divine determinism as well. Predestination requires a divine determination that certain events (eternal salvation) will come to pass. Ensuring that that decree is actualized in a way that fits the complexities of individual personal histories may in turn require other acts of grace, but it does not require global determinism.

Even without determinism, predestination raises complex questions about the relationship between God and evil. Evil is clearly contrary to God's commands, but a God who knows and shapes ultimate destinies in a fallen world can hardly help but permit a good deal of evil. Various kinds of evil may even be incorporated into the divine plan. For instance, if God predestines human beings for redemption, this seems to imply accepting that they will have experiences or conditions from which they need to be redeemed. In addition, if a hell exists that has any sinners in it, it is natural to ask why those creatures would be made by a creator who knows they will experience ultimate disaster. At any rate, even if none are reprobate one may wonder why God permits suffering and other evils to occur in earthly life. A God who makes room for evil, not only knowing it will happen but having set up the context in which it is likely to happen, need not be considered the agent of that evil but nevertheless seems morally accountable for its existence.

Anselm, clearly, was attracted to libertarianism partly because he thought it, with the help of a free will theodicy, could solve the problem of God's relation to sin. His view does not, however, remove divine responsibility for evil. Even on a libertarian view

God is responsible for permitting quite a lot of evil. This is so first because it appears that God could put a stop to evil if God so pleased. Doing so might interfere with human free will (of a libertarian sort), and that might provide God a reason not to do so. If that is a good reason not to interfere, God is not blameworthy for permitting evil. Even so, God is responsible for that decision. Second, God is responsible not just for permitting particular evils but for having created a context in which such evils were likely to occur. Perhaps God could not have created a world without evil, though it is hard to see exactly why that would be the case. At any rate, God could have refused to create. Even if God lacked foreknowledge few monotheists would deny that God was in a position to know that there was a high chance for there to be evil in this world. Thus, God is responsible for having created the context in which evil occurs. Again, God may have a good justification for doing so, and if so God is not to be blamed for having created our world. God may even be praiseworthy! But God is responsible. The appropriate question is what justifies God's relationship to evil.

The free will theodicy argues that God is justified in permitting evil because doing so is necessary for us to have genuinely self-determining choices. Defenders of predestination can respond to this attempt to justify God in at least two ways. First, the possibility of predestination without complete divine determinism, as well as the possibility that libertarian agency is real even if it is rare, suggests that a limited appropriation of a free will theodicy is possible alongside a doctrine of predestination. Even if the ultimate facts about our moral and spiritual lives are predestined, a variety of significant choices between good and evil may have been left up to us. Such a "mixed" approach would allow that the free will theodicy may explain some of the evil in the world.

Second, defenders of predestination who think it better not to make any appeal to libertarianism should press the question of just how much explanatory power the free will theodicy has. The less its explanatory power the lower the cost of giving it up, and the easier it will be to argue that affirming predestination leaves theists no worse off with respect to theodicy than libertarianism.

The free theodicy has some well-known limits. As Marilyn Adams in particular has argued, many evils cannot be justified by an appeal to the value of undetermined free choice.[15] Some evils fall into this category because they seem so large. Genocide is one example. It is not convincing to say that the magnitude of such evils had to be permitted in order to make room for libertarian choices, because such collective evils go far beyond individual choices. Other evils are smaller in scale, but nevertheless not discernably connected to agential motivations. Parents often harm their children without intending to, but surely it is not an expression of free will for them to do so. Consider, too, the many infants and mothers injured or killed by accidents in childbirth. Free will is not relevant to justifying such "natural evils." One could go on in this depressing vein: illness, genetic malfunctions, many natural disasters, and other events out of our control cannot be justified by reference to God's respect for human free will.

The problems of luck discussed above suggest that the category of events outside our control is larger than we typically acknowledge. This undermines the power of free will theodicies. Because of the role chance plays in everyday events large and small, it seems that many evils could be diminished or even avoided, were God so to ordain, without problematically diminishing the import of human choices. One example is the multiple attempts to assassinate Hitler that only barely failed. Had a suitcase been positioned in a slightly different part of the room it would have killed Hitler earlier in World War Two rather than merely wounding him. And why should it not have? One might answer that if God directed the outcomes of our choices that would make them less significant. However, it is difficult to see why it should be more problematic for a well-intentioned God to influence the outcomes of our choices than for luck to do so. Indeed, better God than mere chance, one would think.

Because theists believe that God is properly the giver and taker of life, even a God who respected a wide range of libertarian free choices could end the lives of many evildoers prior to their doing their greatest evils. Short of simply ending a life, God could also disable or delimit various actions via illness, stroke, dementia, and so on. Indeed, the psychological research on situational influences on behavior mentioned above suggests that an imaginative and subtle deity could do a great many other things to influence the course of history. We might ponder, for instance, Herbert Butterfield's reminder that something as small as "the shape of Cleopatra's nose altered the course of history."[16] If the situations and cues that prompt behavior were nudged carefully the guiding hand of history could massively reduce the evil in the world, redirecting human choices without undermining them—much as adults often do with children.

Proponents of the free will theodicy might reply that even if only a small portion of God's permission of evil can be justified by reference to the good of undetermined choice, a free will theodicy offers an incremental advance in dealing with the problem. A partial explanation is better than none at all, and gives us at least some sense of why we can trust God in spite of all the evil in and around us.

However, compatibilist defenders of predestination need feel little sense of loss in abandoning the free will theodicy. That is not simply because of the limitations in explanatory power just explored, but because the entire strategy of justifying evil by appealing to human autonomy seems misguided, in two ways. First, as Augustine may have been the first to contend, undetermined choice is not such a great good that we should invoke it to justify God's permission of serious evils.[17] It is noticeable that we do not think human beings are justified in permitting very significant evils because of the good of respecting free choice. If I see a consenting adult agree to enslavement, I should not respect this choice but rather intervene in some way. We act in the same way in response to any number of more everyday cases of free choice. It is not at all clear, therefore, that God should be praised for a policy of always permitting free choices to go ahead. Even if libertarian self-determination is intrinsically good, its value is not so high that it is preferable to compatibilist forms of personal agency that enable a more loving and less distant relationship between the human and the divine.

Second, it is not at all clear that libertarian self-determination is intrinsically good. Free will theodicies, like libertarianism in general, place a great burden on human agency, making ultimate destinies depend on our choices. Yet much of the time we only half know what we are doing, at best, so it seems unfortunate to place so much weight on what we decide. Often, we do not really understand what we want, or how to get it. Only rarely do we have deep insight into the implications of choosing a particular lover, career, diet, or even shoe. We experience such limitations even more in relation to divine things. It would be better, therefore, if our choices were not fully determinative for us.

Consider, as a test case, a topic widely believed to be a theological strength of libertarianism, the problem of hell. It is sometimes said that hell makes the most sense on libertarianism, because of the heightened degree of responsibility associated with the view and God's inability to direct ultimate destinies. The truth in this claim is that libertarian views do a better job of explaining why God would permit some creatures to reject the offer of union with Christ than compatibilist views. However, hell—at least, as it has traditionally been conceived, as a place of eternal punishment—is not a necessary concomitant of rejecting divine grace. Those who reject the divine offer of eternal life could simply be given no more than the finite existence implied by their creation as creatures whose lives have a beginning and an end.

Libertarian defenders of hell, most prominently Anselm, have dealt with this problem by arguing that eternal punishment is a just response to the infinitely bad evil of rejecting God. That response is flawed in several ways, however. One might readily doubt that rejecting divine grace is infinitely bad. Human beings have, of course, done many very bad things. Yet infinite badness is difficult to rate. Moreover, creaturely choices relating to divine things are, at best, understood only dimly. Do we really think we understand what it means to reject divine grace, or even, in many cases, when we are doing so? In relation to the divine our choices are like that of children. We are not unaccountable for them, but our accountability is diminished by the fact that we lack insight. Those who choose to reject divine grace are deeply ignorant and know not what they do. It is hard to see such choices as paradigmatically free and responsible to the highest degree.

Even if our choices about divine things were well informed and highly responsible, eternal punishment is a response of such great severity that it is difficult to see what would warrant it. We might grant the claim that rejecting God is infinitely bad, but it is not clear what should follow. That should not be surprising, since the implications of claims about infinities are notoriously difficult to assess.

My argument so far has been that distinctively libertarian approaches to the problem of evil are more problematic than is widely assumed. Because of this, defenders of predestination do not lose much in incremental explanatory power by abandoning it to focus on other theodical strategies. Affirming predestination and an associated compatibilist conception of human agency is not noticeably worse from the perspective of theodicy, and may in fact be better. That is true, in part, because nonlibertarians who eschew a free will theodicy can offer other partial justifications of divine goodness, such as the claim that evil is permitted for the sake of great goods like redemption, training in virtue, or other positive developments in personal and salvation history. Developing such claims leaves predestinarians in a position similar to that of theistic libertarians, with some reason to trust in divine goodness but also with a great deal of unexplained evil.

This leads to a further point. Universalist doctrines of predestination offer a powerful avenue for defending divine goodness. If humanity is, as Barth hoped, elected in Christ to participate with God eternally, that is a very great good. Indeed, it is such a great good that it would make every human life worth living regardless of the other details of that life.[18] Every person who receives such a gift has an overriding reason to thank God. Of course, here again many aspects of the problem of evil remain a mystery about which we have only a little that is helpful to say. God might still seem less than perfectly loving for having put us through so much suffering prior to giving us eternal joy. Even once we account for the ways in which permission of sin and other evils can create pedagogical or soteriological opportunities, much of the evil in the world seems unnecessary. Yet it makes a difference to hope that no life is overcome by evil and suffering. If God predestines all for ultimate joy, no life story is finally tragic, and that significantly reframes our view of the role evil plays in the world. Universalist doctrines of predestination, therefore, offer theists a way to make powerful and compelling claims about divine goodness.

Universalist views have become increasingly popular for just such reasons. It is tempting to rest my case at this point, having pointed out that predestination can be defended against the charge that it exacerbates the problem of evil as well as the charge that it undermines human agency. Yet a defense of predestination that links predestination only to universalism would be much weaker than one that is open to a wider range of views. After all, universalism continues to be controversial. This is not simply because Augustinian or other Christians are mean-spirited, but because the entire Christian tradition has taken the idea of hell seriously from its inception. Jesus started this tradition by consistently offering warnings about hell in his parables and discourses. Many theists in other traditions, as well, consider it unduly speculative to rule out the possibility of hell. It makes sense, therefore, to consider what a nonuniversalist compatibilist defender of predestination might say to address questions about divine goodness in relation to hell.

One possibility would be to defend openness to a "wide" account of generous election in which hell exists but is significantly sidelined.

Such a view would offer the possibility that most persons are elect, and the assurance that those in hell want to be there. If they gave up the perversity that separated them from God they, like Dante's Satan, would no longer be in hell. Correlatively, it would make sense to emphasize the nonsadistic nature of hell itself. Some might object that the Bible itself portrays hell as a place of fire and intense, endless suffering. It is notable, however, that the Christian tradition has long taken the image of fire as a general metaphor for punishment, and has as a result taken quite a variety of perspectives on the nature of hell. It has been widely recognized that the sparse biblical references to hell underdetermine particular theologies of hell. This opens up the possibility of hoping that if hell exists it is not the sadistic place of torture made infamous in the portraits of Hieronymus Bosch and others, but more like the thin, near to nonexistent place pictured in C. S. Lewis's *The Great Divorce*. Those who are at odds with their own source of being foolishly prefer hell's shallow pleasures to the difficult and to them inscrutable joys of heaven.[19] Such lives are objectively bad, and presumably subjectively unsatisfying in deep ways. Such a hell is, as it must be, not a happy place. It is not, however, perverse in the way of some traditional pictures of hell. Rather, hell's punishments are a natural outworking of sin, which through false delights imprisons and diminishes the self. On this perspective, hell is in some respects not entirely different from this life, in which sin often exacts a recognizable price from sinners.

Such a "mild" picture of hell is more bearable than the hell of popular imagination, but its eternal duration ensures that it remains a theological puzzle. Why would God decree eternal punishment, even of this relatively humane sort? We may grant the partial persuasiveness of traditional answers, such as Aquinas's claim that God does not owe anyone heaven, or Calvin's argument that God desires to show both justice and mercy. Neither of these claims succeeds in offering a theological rationale for anything more than purgatory, however. Calvin may have been right to claim that God has reason not to send everyone directly to heaven, but demonstration of divine justice hardly seems to require eternal separation from one's creator. Quite a lot of punishment and pedagogy is possible short of that. Aquinas may have been right to claim that God is under no obligation to save, but that does not explain why God would not simply let some finite creatures die and remain dead.

Both replies also fail to deal with the question posed by divine excellence. Even if sending people to hell is not wrong for God, a

larger question remains that should be framed not simply negatively, as the problem of God's relation to evil, but positively, in
terms of God's relation to goodness. On many traditional theistic
metaethics God has no obligations to creatures, but that does not
make all possible divine relationships to creation equally admirable.
God is not merely praised for not violating divine obligations but
for being an exemplar of highest virtue. The question, then, is not
whether God is obligated to redeem but what would be admirable
for that than which none greater can be conceived. Divine goodness
would seem to suggest more generosity and less severity than the
idea of hell implies.

The arguments just offered against a compatibilist depiction of
the fittingness of hell are similar to those employed above against
a libertarian depiction of hell as deserved. On libertarian views we
are more responsible for our sin than on compatibilist views, but
the gaps between Divine goodness, personal responsibility, and
eternal punishment make hell a conundrum for either view. On
both views it is difficult to say why it is good or appropriate for
those who do not love their own source of life to continue to exist
in perpetual suffering. Indeed, the best way to defend a doctrine
of hell on either approach is not to argue that it is morally necessary or fitting for God to punish eternally, but rather to build the
case that those who revere Christian traditions and scripture would
be mistaken if they thought they knew enough to rule it out. This
suggests that adding belief in hell does not change the conclusion
drawn above concerning the general relationship between predestination and the problem of evil. Although it is true that defenders
of predestination are not able to resolve the questions about divine
goodness associated with hell, their belief in predestination does
not necessarily make the problem significantly worse.

In summary, my suggestion is that predestination either helps
with the problem of divine goodness, when it is paired with an
affirmation of universal salvation, or, when paired with a doctrine
of hell, makes the problem not noticeably worse than it already is
on libertarian views. A hopeful universalism like Barth's seems open
to both of these possibilities. On grounds of epistemic humility it
cannot rule hell out, yet it admits that universal salvation seems to
make more theological sense. That may be the best way to offer
hope while eschewing speculation.

6. Conclusion

Although perhaps most theists throughout history believed in pre-destination, it has become difficult for many modern theists to envision how a loving God could predestine. Being destined for a relationship with God before even being born is widely thought to diminish that relationship, because we cannot choose it for ourselves. Upon reflection, however, it becomes clear that the kinds of relationships we actually have and value are not much under our control. In fact, it would be rather odd if they were. Familial and romantic love, most obviously, would not be what they are, were they a matter of choice. Their beauty and poignancy is partly due to the ways in which they come over us, and we find ourselves in them. In these relationships, we love not because we must, but also not because we choose. Indeed, when we must deliberate about our loves, or attempt to will ourselves to love, we do so because we are struggling. Chosen loves may be good at times and for particular reasons, but they are not our preferred or highest states of love. When all is well we love involuntarily, for the reasons that we have, given who we are. Love is evoked by the beauty of the objects of our affection, by the sort of relationship in which we are, and so on. It is thus that our loves both constitute us and express who we are.

Of course, if God were to constitute us as lovers of the divine, against our wills, that would violate us. But God has no need to resort to such brute tactics. For one thing, God is actually beautiful and good, so it is not as though we need to be brainwashed in order to be attracted to a relationship with what is after all divine. Moreover, the divine determination at work in predestining us for life in relation to the Trinity works with us, having shaped us and our deepest yearnings from the beginning, and forming our hopes and beliefs and cares along the way. If Augustine was right we tend to go astray without such support and guidance. On our own we tend to make a mess of others and ourselves, even with what seem to us good intentions. But we were not made to be on our own. We are our best selves in relationships that inspire and lift us up. From that perspective, the idea that God elects us for life in communion seems not an imposition, but a blessing.

NOTES

Introduction

1 See, e.g., Maria De Cillis, *Free Will and Predestination in Islamic Thought: Theoretical Compromises in the Works of Avicenna, al-Ghazali and Ibn 'Arabi* (New York: Routledge, 2013); Jonathan Klawans, *Josephus and the Theologies of Ancient Judaism* (New York: Oxford University Press, 2012), Ch. 2.

2 E.g., Jerry Falwell and Pat Robertson infamously suggested that behind the 9/11 terrorist attacks was God's judgment on the faithlessness of American groups such as gays, lesbians, and the ACLU. For a transcript, see http://www.beliefnet.com/Faiths/Christianity/2001/09/You-Helped-This-Happen.aspx

3 C. S. Lewis, "The Four Loves," in *The Inspirational Writings of C. S. Lewis* (New York: Inspirational Press, 2004), p. 260.

4 Lewis, "The Four Loves," p. 261.

5 Ibid.

6 Ibid.

7 E.g., St. Augustine, *The City of God (XI–XXII)*, Trans. William Babcock, *The Works of Saint Augustine*, I/7 (Hyde Park, NY: New City Press, 2013), XXII.1. Augustine clarified that he did not presume the number of predestined human beings to be limited to the number of fallen angels, though he granted the possibility.

8 Dante Aligheri, *The Inferno*, Trans. Robert Hollander and Jean Hollander (New York: Anchor, 2002), Canto 34.

9 On the connection between autonomy and evil, see Iris Murdoch's incisive comment that Kant's free man was incarnated in the person of Milton's Lucifer in Iris Murdoch, *The Sovereignty of Good* (New York: Routledge, 1970), p. 78.

10 This idea is most famously recounted in *Paradise Lost* (John Milton, *Paradise Lost*, ed. Barbara K. Lewalski (New York: Blackwell, 2007)), but it was also a widespread belief of ancient Jewish and Christian interpreters of the scripture. See, for instance, the *Life of Adam and Eve* in *The Life of Adam and Eve and Related Literature*, ed. Marinus de Jonge and Johannes Tromp (Sheffield, UK: Sheffield Academic Press, 1997). Note that this explanation for the primal sin really just pushes the issue of how good beings could fall into sin back a step—we can still ask how such beings would have become jealous. This suggests that even the best attempts to render the primal sin intelligible remain incomplete.

11 I trace this idea back to the thought of Anselm of Canterbury in the second chapter of the present book, though one could find its earlier roots in the

Pelagian debates, and perhaps even prior to that in the thought of the influential early Christian philosopher Origen.

12 For an influential recent articulation of the idea that human and divine agency are not in competition, see Kathryn Tanner, *God and Creation in Christian Theology: Tyranny or Empowerment?* (Minneapolis, MN: Fortress Press, 2004), pp. 84–104.

13 Arthur C. Clarke, *Childhood's End* (New York: Ballantine Books, 1953), p. 23.

14 St. Augustine, *The Predestination of the Saints*, ed. John E. Rotelle, O. S. A., Trans. Roland J. Teske, S. J., *The Works of Saint Augustine*, Vol. I/26, *Answer to the Pelagians IV* (Hyde Park, NY: New City Press, 1999), 17.34.

15 Friedrich Schleiermacher, *On the Doctrine of Election, with Special Reference to the Aphorisms of Dr. Bretschneider*, Trans. Iain G. Nicol Tice, Jorgenson Allen, and N. Terrence (Louisville, KY: Westminster John Knox Press, 2012).

16 See, for instance, the history of the Puritan debates about predestination in Peter J. Thuesen, *Predestination: The American Career of a Contentious Doctrine* (New York: Oxford University Press, 2009).

Chapter 1

1 For a more thorough discussion of these issues, see Jesse Couenhoven, *Stricken by Sin, Cured by Christ: Agency, Necessity, and Culpability in Augustinian Theology* (New York: Oxford Unversity Press, 2013), Ch. 1.

2 Matthew Levering, *Predestination: Biblical and Theological Paths* (New York: Oxford University Press, 2011), p. 19.

3 For a longer discussion of this topic than I offer here, see Levering, *Predestination: Biblical and Theological Paths*, Ch. 1.

4 For a list of passages that Augustine considered particularly telling, see *The Predestination of the Saints*. Trans. Roland J. Teske, S. J. *The Works of Saint Augustine*, Vol. I/26, *Answer to the Pelagians IV*, ed. John E. Rotelle, O. S. A. Hyde Park, NY: New City Press, 1999, 2.4–3.7. Citations to Augustine's works are to chapters and sections in his books, not to page numbers.

5 Augustine, *Predestination*, 3.7.

6 See Augustine, *The Gift of Perseverance*. Trans. Roland J. Teske, S. J. *The Works of Saint Augustine*, Vol. I/26, *Answer to the Pelagians IV*, ed. John E. Rotelle, O. S. A. Hyde Park, NY: New City Press, 1999, 9.22–23.

7 I comment further on this topic in Jesse Couenhoven, "Augustine, Saint," in *International Encyclopedia of Ethics*, Hugh LaFollette (Malden, MA: Blackwell Press, 2013), pp. 1–3.

8 At least to some degree, Augustine admits this himself. See Augustine, *Perseverence*, 21.55.

9 Augustine, *Predestination*, 12.23.

10 Augustine, *Perseverence*, 14.35.

11 Augustine, *Predestination*, 15.31.

12 Augustine, *Perseverence*, 24.67.

13 Jn 15:16; see the repeated reference to this verse in Augustine, *Predestination*, 17.34. Augustine clearly considers this saying an encapsulated form of the

repeated story in scripture that began with God choosing Israel among the nations, not because of its greatness but in order to make it great.

14 Augustine, *Perseverance*, 24.67. In his *Unfinished Work in Answer to Julian*, ed. John E. Rotelle, O. S. A., Trans. Roland J. Teske, S. J., *Answer to the Pelagians, III Vol. I/25* (Hyde Park, NY: New City Press), IV.134. Augustine suggests that Jeremiah and John the Baptist fit this pattern, too. Both exemplify the prevenience of divine grace, which is why Jeremiah 1:4–5 says that "before I formed you in the womb, I knew you, before you were born I set you apart; I appointed you as a prophet to the nations."

15 Augustine, *Predestination*, 12.23.

16 See, for instance, Augustine's discussion in *Perseverance*, 22.57–61.

17 Augustine, *Perseverance*, 62.61.

18 For more on this topic, see Jesse Couenhoven, "Augustine's Rejection of the Free Will Defence: An Overview of the late Augustine's Theodicy," *Religious Studies* 43 (2007).

19 Augustine, *Predestination*, 21.54.

20 See Augustine, *Perseverence*, 15.38–16.39.

21 See Paul Russell, "Compatibilist-Fatalism," in *Moral Responsibility and Ontology*, ed. Ton van den Beld (Boston, MA: Kluwer Academic Publishers, 2000) for a helpful discussion of what a compatibilist has in mind when saying that her or his view is not fatalist.

22 I consider a different take on divine foreknowledge and its relationship to predestination in the discussion of Anselm in the following chapter.

23 See, for instance, Gerald Bonner, *Freedom and Necessity: St. Augustine's Teaching on Divine Power and Human Freedom* (Washington, DC: The Catholic University of America Press, 2007), pp. 1–2.

24 I have offered more technical discussions of a number of the issues discussed below in other places, including Couenhoven, *Stricken by Sin*, Ch. 3, and "The Necessities of Perfect Freedom," *International Journal of Systematic Theology* 14, no. 4 (2012).

25 St. Augustine, *The City of God*, William Babcock, *The Works of Saint Augustine, I/6* (Hyde Park, NY: New City Press, 2012), V.10.

26 Augustine, *Predestination*, 8.13.

27 Ibid., 10.19.

28 Augustine, *City of God*, V.9.

29 Augustine, *Predestination*, 10.19.

30 John Dunne, ed. *Poems of John Donne*. Vol. I. (London: Lawrence & Bullen, 1896), "Holy Sonnet XIV."

31 See Augustine, *City of God*, V.9.

32 Augustine, *Predestination*, 3.7.

33 For Augustine's comments on prayer in relation to predestination, see Augustine, *Perseverance*, 2.3–7.15.

34 St. Augustine, *Rebuke and Grace*. Trans. Roland J. Teske. *The Works of Saint Augustine, Vol. I/26, Answer to the Pelagians IV*, ed. John E. Rotelle, O. S. A. (Hyde Park, NY: New City Press, 1999), 3.5 and 5.7–6.9.

35 Augustine, *Predestination*, 6.11.

36 St. Augustine, *Grace and Free Choice*. Trans. Roland J. Teske. *The Works of Saint Augustine, Vol. I/26, Answer to the Pelagians IV*, ed. John E. Rotelle, O. S. A. (Hyde Park, NY: New City Press, 1999), 3.5.

37   For a representative passage, see Augustine, *Rebuke and Grace*, 8.17.
38   Augustine, *Grace and Free Choice*, 20.41.
39   Ibid., 2.4.

Chapter 2

1   See St. Augustine, *The City of God*, Trans. William Babcock. *The Works of Saint Augustine*, I/6 (Hyde Park, NY: New City Press, 2012), XV.7.
2   See Anselm, *De Concordia (The Compatibility of God's Foreknowledge, Predestination, and Grace with Human Freedom)*, ed. Brian Davies and G. R. Evans, Trans. Thomas Bermingham, *Anselm of Canterbury: The Major Works* (New York: Oxford University Press, 1998), p. 471. See also Anslem, *On the Fall of the Devil*, Trans. Ralph McInerny. *Anselm of Canterbury: The Major Works*, ed. Brian Davies and G. R. Evans (New York: Oxford University Press, 1998), pp. 216–17.
3   Augustine, *Unfinished Work in Answer to Julian*. Trans. Roland J. Teske, S. J. *Answer to the Pelagians, III. Vol. I/25, VI.32.* ed. John E. Rotelle, O. S. A. (Hyde Park, NY: New City Press, 1999).
4   Anselm, *On Free Will*, Trans. Ralph McInerny. *Anselm of Canterbury: The Major Works*, ed. Brian Davies and G. R. Evans (New York: Oxford University Press, 1998), p. 179.
5   See Anslem, *On the Fall of the Devil*. It is not entirely clear why angels are given just one chance, but it was widely thought before and after Anselm's time that scripture teaches that no fallen angels are redeemed. Philosophically, it may have seemed significant that the angels are purely rational creatures who can go "all in" on their choices in ways that human beings, composed as they are of body and spirit, cannot. The purity of their choice might also be sullied if they were given an opportunity to make it over again, having, so to speak, tested the waters.
6   For a good, brief discussion, see Sandra Visser, "Anselm of Canterbury," in *The Routledge Companion to Free Will*, ed. Neil Levy, Meghan Griffith, and Kevin Timpe (New York: Routledge, 2016).
7   Anselm, *On Free Will*, p. 179.
8   Ibid., p. 176.
9   Anselm, *On the Fall of the Devil*, p. 227.
10 Anselm, *De Concordia*, pp. 449–50.
11 See Katherin Rogers, *Anselm on Freedom* (New York: Oxford University Press, 2008), Ch. 7 for a perceptive discussion of these issues.
12 To keep things simple, I am ignoring the complex options later offered by Ockham, Molina, and others. For an overview of some of the relevant issues, see James K. and Paul R. Eddy Beilby, eds. *Divine Foreknowledge: Four Views* (Downers Grove, IL: InterVarsity Press, 2001).
13 For a now classic articulation of the view, see John Sanders, *The God Who Risks: A Theology of Providence* (Downers Grove, IL: InterVarsity Press, 1998), and for a recent more technical discussion, William Hasker, *Providence, Evil, and the Openness of God* (New York: Routledge, 2004).

Chapter 3

1 Thomas Aquinas, *Summa Theologica*, Trans. Fathers of the English Dominican Province (New York: Benzinger Brothers, 1947), I.23.1. Citations of Aquinas's works are by part and question numbers, not page numbers.
2 Aquinas, *Summa Theologica*, I.23.2.
3 On the distinction between willing not to act and not willing to act, see *Summa Theologica*, I–II.6.3.
4 Aquinas, *Summa Theologica*, I.23.3.
5 Ibid., I.23.4 r3.
6 Ibid., III.24.3.
7 Ibid., III.24.4.
8 Thomas Aquinas, *On Evil*, Trans. Jean Osterle (Notre Dame, IN: University of Notre Dame Press, 1995), IV.5.
9 Aquinas, *Summa Theologica*, I–II, 6.1.
10 Ibid., I–II 9, 10.
11 Aquinas, *On Evil*, VI.
12 God might be said to have intellect and will but only analogously, because in God all things are one and God has no separate powers.
13 Aquinas, *Summa Theologica*, I–II 6.1–2.
14 Aquinas, *On Evil*, VI (p. 243).
15 See Robert Pasnau, *Thomas Aquinas on Human Nature* (New York: Cambridge University Press, 2002), Ch. 7 for an insightful compatibilist reading, and Eleonore Stump, *Aquinas* (New York: Routledge, 2005), Ch. 9 for a nuanced libertarian reading.
16 See Tobias Hoffman and Peter Furlong, "Free Choice," in *Aquinas's Disputed Questions on Evil: A Critical Guide*, M. V. ed. Dougherty (New York: Cambridge University Press, 2015), p. 62.
17 Aquinas, *Summa Theologica*, I.83.3.
18 Ibid., I.83.3 and III.18.4.
19 Ibid., III.18.4 r3.
20 Ibid., I.83.1.
21 Ibid.
22 Ibid., I–II.15.4 r2.
23 Ibid., I.19.8.
24 For example, see Aquinas, *Summa Theologica*, I–II.13.6.
25 Aquinas, *Summa Theologica*, I.19.3.

Chapter 4

1 Martin Luther, *Lectures on Romans*, ed. Jaroslav Pelican, Trans. Walter G. Tillmanns and Jacob A. O. Preus, *Luther's Works Vol. 25* (Saint Louis, MO: Concordia Publishing House, 1972), p. 371.
2 Martin Luther, *The Bondage of the Will*, ed. Helmut T. Lehmann, Trans. Philip S. Watson and Benjamin Drewery, *Luther's Works, Career of the Reformer*

III: Vol 33 (Philadelphia, PA: Fortress Press, 1972), p. 40. See also *Romans*, p. 372.

3 "Heidelberg Disputation," in *Luther's Works, Volume 31: Career of the Reformer I*, ed. Helmut T. Lehmann and Harold J. Grimm (Philadelphia, PA: Fortress Press, 1957), p. 41.

4 See, for instance, Luther's "Disputation Against Scholastic Theology." Trans. Harold J. Grimm. In *Luther's Works, Volume 31: Career of the Reformer I*, ed. Helmut T. Lehmann and Harold J. Grimm (Philadelphia, PA: Fortress Press, 1957).

5 As we will see, Calvin was more appreciative of Aristotle, whose ideas he appropriated eclectically.

6 Cf. Robert Kolb, *Bound Choice, Election, and Wittenberg Theological Method: From Martin Luther to the Formula of Concord* (Grand Rapids, MI: William B. Eerdmans Publishing Company, 2005), p. 19.

7 Martin Luther, *Lectures on Galations 1535: Chapters 1–4*, ed. and Trans. Jaroslav Pelican, *Luther's Works, Vol 26* (Saint Louis, MI: Concordia Publishing House, 1963), p. 91. See Gilbert Meilaender, "The Examined Life is Not Worth Living: Learning from Luther," in *The Theory and Practice Of Virtue* (South Bend, IN: University of Notre Dame Press, 1988) for illuminating commentary.

8 Luther, *Galations*, p. 169.

9 See Luther, *Bondage*, p. 187.

10 Ibid., p. 40.

11 Ibid., p. 214.

12 Ibid., p. 371.

13 Ibid., p. 43.

14 Ibid., pp. 36ff, 184ff.

15 Ibid., p. 37.

16 Ibid., p. 373.

17 Ibid., pp. 185, 193–5.

18 Ibid., p. 190. Luther described this as a distinction between the ordinary and absolute will of God, but the point he was rejecting is the same.

19 Luther, *Bondage*, p. 192.

20 Martin Luther, *Lectures on Genesis*, ed. Jaroslav Pelican, Trans. George V. Schick and Paul D. Pahl, *Luther's Works Vol. 5* (Saint Louis, MO: Concordia Publishing House, 1968), pp. 42–50.

21 See, for example, Robert Kolb, *Bound Choice, Election, and Wittenberg Theological Method: From Martin Luther to the Formula of Concord* (Grand Rapids, MI: William B. Eerdmans Publishing Company, 2005), especially Ch. 1. For an overview of recent attempts to make sense of Luther's view, see Piotr J. Małysz, "Martin Luther's Trinitarian Hermeneutic of Freedom," in *Oxford Research Encyclopedia of Religion*, ed. John Barton (New York: Oxford University Press, 2017).

22 Martin Luther, "Letter to Wolfgang Capito, July 9, 1537," in *Luther's Works, Vol 50. Letters III.*, ed. Helmut T. Lehmann (Philadelphia, PA: Fortress Press, 1974), pp. 172–3.

23 For a summary of the role these terms play in Augustine's thought, see Jesse Couenhoven, "Augustine of Hippo," in *The Routledge Companion to Free Will*, Kevin Timpe, Meghan Griffith, and Neil Levy (New York: Routledge, 2016).

24 Cf. Luther, "Heidelberg Disputation," pp. 50–1.

25 Luther, *Bondage*, p. 65.

26 Ibid., p. 272. Such claims are not limited to this text. See, for instance, Luther's "Disputation Against Scholastic Theology," p. 9; "Heidelberg Disputation," p. 40.

27 On this point, Luther parted from Augustine, who considered pride and sloth more basic forms of human sin.

28 Luther, *Bondage*, p. 103.

29 Ibid., p. 70.

30 Ibid., p. 70.

31 Ibid., p. 103, cf. 69.

32 Ibid., p. 64.

33 Ibid., p. 67.

34 Ibid., pp. 39, 65.

35 Ibid., p. 243.

36 This is the argument in *The Freedom of a Christian*, ed. John Dillenberger, Trans. W. A. Lambert and Revised by Harold J. Grimm, *Martin Luther, Selections from His Writings* (Philadelphia, PA: Fortress Press, 1951), pp. 42–85.

37 Luther, *Bondage*, pp. 201–2.

38 Ibid., p. 196.

39 John Calvin, *Institutes of the Christian Religion*, ed. John T. McNeill, Trans. Ford Lewis Battles, *The Library of Christian Classics, Vol. 20* (Philadelphia, PA: The Westminster Press, 1960), III.XXIII.4.

40 Calvin, *Institutes*, III.XXI.5.

41 Ibid.

42 Calvin, *Institutes*, III.XXI.6–7.

43 Calvin, *Institutes*, III.XXIII.1.

44 John Calvin, *Concerning the Eternal Predestination of God*, Trans. J. K. S. Reid (Louisville, KY: Westminster John Knox Press, 1997), p. 174.

45 Calvin, *Predestination*, p. 108.

46 Calvin, *Institutes*, III.23.6.

47 Ibid.

48 Calvin, *Predestination*, p. 177.

49 Ibid., p. 170.

50 Ibid., p. 169.

51 Ibid., pp. 177–8.

52 John Calvin, *The Bondage and Liberation of the Will: A Defence of the Orthodox Doctrine of Human Choice Against Pighius*, ed. A. N. S. Lane, Trans. Graham I. Davies (Grand Rapids, MI: Baker Books, 1996), pp. 47, 92.

53 Calvin, *Bondage and Liberation*, p. 68.

54 Ibid., pp. 69, 148.

55 Ibid., p. 147.

56 Ibid., p. 149.

57 Ibid., p. 41.

58 Ibid., p. 213.

59 Ibid., p. 226.

60 Ibid., p. 232.

61 Calvin, *Predestination*, p. 181.

62 For helpful discussion of Calvin's views see Paul Helm, "Calvin the Compatibilist," in *Calvin at the Centre* (New York: Oxford University Press, 2010) and *John Calvin's Ideas* (New York: Oxford University Press, 2004), Ch. 6.

63 Calvin, *Predestination*, pp. 168–82.

64 See, for example, Calvin, *Institutes*, II.2.25.

65 *Institutes*, III.23.7.

Chapter 5

1 Karl Barth, *Church Dogmatics, II/2*, ed. G. W. Bromily and T. F. Torrance, Trans. G. W. Bromily, J. C. Cambell, Iain Wilson, J. Strathern McNab, Harold Knight, and R. A. Stewart (Edinburgh: T&T Clark, 1957), pp. 13–14. Citations throughout this chapter refer to the *Church Dogmatics* as *CD*, followed by part and volume numbers, and then page numbers.

2 Barth, *CD II/2*, p. 111.

3 See, for example, John Calvin, *Concerning the Eternal Predestination of God.* Trans. J. K. S. Reid. (Louisville, KY: Westminster John Knox Press, 1997), p. 113.

4 Barth, *CD II/2*, pp. 39–41.

5 Ibid., p. 143; cf. 70–76.

6 Ibid., p. 162.

7 Ibid., p. 167; cf. 353.

8 Ibid., p. 167.

9 Ibid., p. 162.

10 The reading of Barth offered in this chapter has learned from George Hunsinger, *Reading Barth with Charity: A Hermeneutical Proposal* (Grand Rapids, MI: Baker Academic, 2015), and Kevin W. Hector, "God's Triunity and Self-Determination: A Conversation with Karl Barth, Bruce McCormack and Paul Molnar," *International Journal of Systematic Theology* 7, no. 3, 2005.

11 Karl Barth, *Church Dogmatics, III/3*, ed. G. W. Bromily and T. F. Torrance, Trans. G. W. Bromily and R. J. Ehrlich (Edinburgh: T&T Clark, 1960), pp. 4–5.

12 See, e.g., Barth, *CD II/2*, pp. 3–4.

13 Ibid., p. 101.

14 See *Christ and Adam: Man and Humanity in Romans 5* (New York: Harper, 1957).

15 Barth, *CD II/2*, p. 94.

16 Revelations 13:8.

17 See, for instance, Ephesians 1:4–5, 11, and 3:11, and Hebrews 1:1–3.

18 Barth, *CD II/2*, p. 102.

19 *Church Dogmatics, IV/2*, ed. G. W. Bromiley and T. F. Torrance, Trans. G. W. Bromiley (Edinburgh: T&T Clark, 1958), p. 64.

20 Barth, *CD IV/2*, p. 59.

21 Ibid., p. 69.

22 This theme is pervasive, but see for instance *Church Dogmatics, II/1*, ed. G. W. Bromily and T. F. Torrance, Trans. T. H. L. Parker, W. B. Johnston, Harold Knight, and J. L. M. Haire (Edinburgh: T&T Clark, 1957), pp. 273–80 and *CD II/2*, pp. 9–10.

23 *Church Dogmatics, III/1*, ed. G. W. Bromily and T. F. Torrance, Trans. G. W. Bromily (Edinburgh: T&T Clark, 1970), pp. 231–2.

24 Barth, *CD II/2*, p. 10.

25 Ibid., p. 44.

26 *Church Dogmatics, IV/3.2*, ed. G. W. Bromiley and T. F. Torrance, Trans. G. W. Bromiley (Edinburgh: T&T Clark, 1962), p. 528.

27 Barth, *CD II/2*, p. 179.

28 Ibid., pp. 548, 550, and 175, respectively.

29 See, e.g., Barth, *CD II/2*, p. 177; and *Church Dogmatics, III/2*, ed. G. W. Bromily and T. F. Torrance, Trans. G. W. Bromily, Harold Knight, J. K. S. Reid, and R. H. Fuller (Edinburgh: T&T Clark, 1960), p. 180.

30 See, e.g., *CD III/3*, pp. 120–21.

31 *CD IV/3.2*, p. 491.

32 Ibid., p. 942.

33 *CD II/2*, p. 30.

34 *CD III/3*, p. 119.

35 *CD II/2*, p. 301.

36 For a more sustained discussion of these issues see Jesse Couenhoven, "Karl Barth's Conception(s) of Human and Divine Freedom(s)," in *Commanding Grace: Studies in Barth's Ethics*, ed. Daniel Migliore (Grand Rapids, MI: William B. Eerdmans, 2010).

37 John Godsey, ed. *Karl Barth's Table Talk* (Richmond, VA: John Knox Press, 1963), p. 37. Cf. Barth, *CD III/3*, p. 150.

38 *The Christian Life: Church Dogmatics Volume IV, Part 4, Lecture Fragments*, Trans. Geoffrey W. Bromiley (Grand Rapids, MI: William B. Eerdmans, 1981), p. 4.

39 See, e.g., *Church Dogmatics, IV/1*, ed. G. W. Bromiley and T. F. Torrance, Trans. G. W. Bromiley (Edinburgh: T&T Clark, 1956), p. 746.

40 Godsey, *Barth's Table Talk*, p. 150.

41 Barth, *CD II/2*, p. 178, cf. 179–80.

42 *Christian Life*, p. 941.

43 *CD III/3*, pp. 118, 136.

44 *CD II/2*, p. 29.

45 *CD III/3*, pp. 133–4. I think it is fair to say that few theologians have found this worry compelling.

46 *CD IV/3.2*, p. 548. See also, for example, *CD III/3*, pp. 92, 247–8.

47 *CD IV/I*, p. 746.

48 Ibid., p. 747.

49 *CD IV/2*, p. 70.

50 *CD IV/2*, p. 71.

51 *CD III/3*, p. 232.

52 *CD IV/3.2*, p. 665.

53 Ibid.

54 Barth, *CD III/3*, p. 247.

55 *CD III/2*, p. 180.

56 *Christian Life*, p. 44.

57 Ibid., p. 90.

58 Ibid., pp. 263–4.

59 *CD II/2*, pp. 140–2.

60 Ibid., p. 458.
61 *CD II/1*, p. 594.
62 Ibid., p. 595.
63 *CD II/2*, p. 460.
64 Ibid., p. 459.
65 Ibid., pp. 466–7.
66 Ibid., pp. 470–1.
67 Ibid., p, 476.
68 Ibid., p. 496.
69 See, e.g., *CD II/2*, p. 350.
70 Ibid., p. 502.
71 Ibid., p. 504.
72 *Church Dogmatics, IV/3.1*, ed. G. W. Bromiley and T. F. Torrance, Trans. G. W. Bromiley (Edinburgh: T&T Clark, 1961), p. 478.
73 *Christian Life*, p. 271.

Chapter 6

1 Aquinas, *Summa Theologica*, Trans. Fathers of the English Dominican Province (New York: Benzinger Brothers), I.23.2.
2 Robert Pasnau, "Snatching Hope from the Jaws of Epistemic Defeat," *Journal of the American Philosophical Association* 1, no. 2, 2015: 270–3. I am indebted to conversations with Pasnau and Andrew Chignell on the relation of belief and hope.
3 Thomas Nagel, "Moral Luck," in *Mortal Questions* (New York: Cambridge University Press, 1979).
4 See Jesse Couenhoven, *Stricken by Sin, Cured by Christ: Agency, Necessity, and Culpability in Augustinian Theology* (New York: Oxford University Press, 2013), Ch. 5 for development of this view. A somewhat similar philosophical account is offered in T. M. Scanlon, "Reasons and Passions," in *The Contours of Agency*, ed. Sarah Buss and Lee Overton (Cambridge, MA: The MIT Press, 2002).
5 For a thoughtful discussion, see Christian B. Miller, *Character and Moral Psychology* (New York: Oxford University Press, 2014), Ch. 3.
6 See Robert Merrihew Adams, *A Theory of Virtue: Excellence in Being for the Good* (New York: Oxford University Press, 2006), Ch. 8–9 for discussion of these and other cases.
7 Seminal work on this topic was done by Ellen J. Langer, "The Illusion of Control," *Journal of Personality and Social Psychology* 32, no. 2, 1975. For a brief updated perspective on the now voluminous literature, see Suzanne C. Thompson, "Illusions of Control: How We Overestimate Our Personal Influence," *Current Directions in Psychological Science* 8, 1999.
8 Divine foreknowledge may very well point in the same direction, since at least at first glance the idea that God knows that I will do x implies that I must do x, lest God be wrong.

9 My development of this point draws on John Martin Fischer's defense of compatibilism as particularly resilient in John Martin Fischer, Robert Kane, Derk Pereboom, and Manuel Vargas, *Four Views on Free Will* (Malden, MA: Blackwell, 2007), pp. 46–7.

10 For a helpful overview see Kevin Timpe, *Free Will: Sourcehood and Its Alternatives* (New York: Continuum, 2008).

11 Peter van Inwagen, "When the Will is Not Free," *Philosophical Studies* 75, 1994: 108–9. See also Ishtiyaque Haji, *Moral Appraisability: Puzzles, Proposals, and Perplexities* (New York: Oxford University Press, 1998), Ch. 12.

12 See Gary Watson, "Responsibility and the Limits of Evil: Variations on a Strawsonian Theme," in *Responsibility, Character, and the Emotions*, ed. Ferdinand Schoeman (New York: Cambridge University Press, 1987), p. 281, for a rare reference to this issue in the philosophical literature on responsibility. Eugene Schlossberger, *Moral Responsibility and Persons* (Philadelphia, PA: Temple University Press, 1992), pp. 132–6, takes up the topic at some length.

13 This claim is further developed in Lynn Rudder Baker, "Why Christians Should not be Libertarians: An Augustinian Challenge," *Faith and Philosophy* 20, no. 4, 2003.

14 For a thoughtful defense of theological determinism, see Derk Pereboom, "Theological Determinism and the Relationship with God," in *Free Will and Classical Theism: The Significance of Freedom in Perfect Being Theology*, Hugh J. McCann (New York: Oxford University Press, 2017).

15 Marilyn McCord Adams, *Horrendous Evils and the Goodness of God* (Ithaca, NY: Cornell University Press, 1999), Ch. 1.

16 Herbert Butterfield, *Christianity and History* (London: Fontana Books, 1958), p. 145.

17 I develop this point further in Jesse Couenhoven, "Augustine's Rejection of the Free Will Defence: An Overview of the late Augustine's Theodicy," *Religious Studies* 43, 2007.

18 Here I am drawing on Adams, *Horrendous Evils and the Goodness of God*.

19 C. S. Lewis, *The Great Divorce* (New York: HarperOne, 2009). For another fascinating thought experiment about hell, see Ted Chiang, "Hell is the Absence of God," in *Stories of Your Life and Others* (New York: Vintage Books, 2002).

FURTHER READING

Boettner, Lorraine. *The Reformed Doctrine of Predestination.* Phillipsburg, NJ: Presbyterian and Reformed Publishing Company. Original edition, 1932, reprinted 1991.

Cary, Phillip. "Augustinian Compatibilism and the Doctrine of Election." In *Augustine and Philosophy*, Edited by Phillip Cary, John Doody, and Kim Paffenroth, 79–102. Lanham, MD: Lexington Books, 2010.

Cillis, Maria De. *Free Will and Predestination in Islamic Thought: Theoretical Compromises in the Works of Avicenna, al-Ghazali and Ibn 'Arabi.* New York: Routledge, 2013.

Flint, Thomas P. "Two Accounts of Providence." In *Divine and Human Action: Essays in the Metaphysics of Theism*, Edited by Thomas V. Morris, 147–81. Ithaca, NY: Cornell University Press, 1988.

Goris, Harm. "Divine Foreknowledge, Providence, Predestination, and Human Freedom." In *The Theology of Thomas Aquinas*, Edited by Rik Van Nieuwenhove and Joseph P. Wawrykow, 99–122. South Bend, IN: University of Notre Dame Press, 2010.

Leibniz, G. W. *Dissertation on Predestination and Grace.* Translated by Michael J. Murray. New Haven, CT: Yale University Press, 2011.

Levering, Matthew. *Predestination: Biblical and Theological Paths.* New York: Oxford University Press, 2011.

Lloyd, Genevieve. *Providence Lost.* Cambridge, MA: Harvard University Press, 2008.

Long, Steven A., Roger W. Nutt, and Thomas Joseph White, ed. *Thomism and Predestination.* Washington, DC: Catholic University of America Press, 2017.

Schleiermacher, Friedrich. *On the Doctrine of Election, with Special Reference to the Aphorisms of Dr. Bretschneider.* Translated by Iain G. Nicol, and Allen G. Jorgenson. Louisville, KY: Westminster John Knox Press, 2012.

Thuesen, Peter J. *Predestination: The American Career of a Contentious Doctrine.* New York: Oxford University Press, 2009.

Wetzel, James. "Predestination, Pelagianism, and Foreknowledge." In *Cambridge Companion to Augustine*, Edited by Eleonore Stump and Norman Kretzman, 49–58. New York: Cambridge University Press, 2001.

REFERENCES

Adams, Marilyn McCord. *Horrendous Evils and the Goodness of God.* Ithaca, NY: Cornell University Press, 1999.

Adams, Robert Merrihew. *A Theory of Virtue: Excellence in Being for the Good.* New York: Oxford University Press, 2006.

Aligheri, Dante. *The Inferno.* Translated by Robert Hollander and Jean Hollander. New York: Anchor, 2002.

Anselm. *De Concordia (The Compatibility of God's Foreknowledge, Predestination, and Grace with Human Freedom).* Translated by Thomas Bermingham. *Anselm of Canterbury: The Major Works.* Edited by Brian Davies and G. R. Evans. New York: Oxford University Press, 1998.

Anselm. *On Free Will.* Translated by Ralph McInerny. *Anselm of Canterbury: The Major Works.* Edited by Brian Davies and G. R. Evans. New York: Oxford University Press, 1998.

Anselm. *On the Fall of the Devil.* Translated by Ralph McInerny. *Anselm of Canterbury: The Major Works.* Edited by Brian Davies and G. R. Evans. New York: Oxford University Press, 1998.

Aquinas, Thomas. *On Evil.* Translated by Jean Osterle. Notre Dame, IN: University of Notre Dame Press, 1995.

Aquinas, Thomas. *Summa Theologica.* Translated by Fathers of the English Dominican Province. New York: Benzinger Brothers, 1947.

Augustine, St. *The City of God.* Translated by William Babcock. *The Works of Saint Augustine, I/6.* Hyde Park, NY: New City Press, 2012.

Augustine, St. *The City of God (XI–XXII).* Translated by William Babcock. *The Works of Saint Augustine, I/7.* Hyde Park, NY: New City Press, 2013.

Augustine, St. *The Confessions.* Translated by Maria Boulding, O. S. B. Edited by John E. Rotelle, O. S. A. Hyde Park, NY: New City Press, 1997.

Augustine, St. *The Gift of Perseverance.* Translated by Roland J. Teske, S. J. *The Works of Saint Augustine, Vol. I/26, Answer to the Pelagians IV.* Edited by John E. Rotelle, O. S. A. Hyde Park, NY: New City Press, 1999.

Augustine, St. *Grace and Free Choice.* Translated by Roland J. Teske. *The Works of Saint Augustine, Vol. I/26, Answer to the Pelagians IV.* Edited by John E. Rotelle, O. S. A. Hyde Park, NY: New City Press, 1999.

Augustine, St. *The Predestination of the Saints*. Translated by Roland J. Teske, S. J. *The Works of Saint Augustine, Vol. I/26, Answer to the Pelagians IV*. Edited by John E. Rotelle, O. S. A. Hyde Park, NY: New City Press, 1999.

Augustine, St. *Rebuke and Grace*. Translated by Roland J. Teske. *The Works of Saint Augustine, Vol. I/26, Answer to the Pelagians IV*. Edited by John E. Rotelle, O. S. A. Hyde Park, NY: New City Press, 1999.

Augustine, St. *Unfinished Work in Answer to Julian*. Translated by Roland J. Teske, S. J. *Answer to the Pelagians, III*. Vol. I/25, Edited by John E. Rotelle, O. S. A. Hyde Park, NY: New City Press, 1999.

Baker, Lynn Rudder. "Why Christians Should Not Be Libertarians: An Augustinian Challenge." *Faith and Philosophy* 20, no. 4 (2003): 260–78.

Barth, Karl. *Christ and Adam: Man and Humanity in Romans 5*. New York: Harper, 1957.

Barth, Karl. *The Christian Life: Church Dogmatics Volume IV, Part 4, Lecture Fragments*. Translated by Geoffrey W. Bromiley Grand Rapids, MI: William B. Eerdmans, 1981.

Barth, Karl. *Church Dogmatics, II/1*. Translated by T. H. L. Parker, W. B. Johnston, Harold Knight, and J. L. M. Haire. Edited by G. W. Bromily and T. F. Torrance. Edinburgh: T&T Clark, 1957.

Barth, Karl. *Church Dogmatics, II/2*. Translated by G. W. Bromily, J. C. Cambell, Iain Wilson, J. Strathern McNab, Harold Knight, and R. A. Stewart. Edited by G. W. Bromily and T. F. Torrance. Edinburgh: T&T Clark, 1957.

Barth, Karl. *Church Dogmatics, III/1*. Translated by G. W. Bromily. Edited by G. W. Bromily and T. F. Torrance. Edinburgh: T& T Clark, 1970.

Barth, Karl. *Church Dogmatics, III/2*. Translated by G. W. Bromily, Harold Knight, J. K. S. Reid, and R. H. Fuller. Edited by G. W. Bromily and T. F. Torrance. Edinburgh: T&T Clark, 1960.

Barth, Karl. *Church Dogmatics, III/3*. Translated by G. W. Bromily and R. J. Ehrlich. Edited by G. W. Bromily and T. F. Torrance. Edinburgh: T&T Clark, 1960.

Barth, Karl. *Church Dogmatics, IV/1*. Translated by G. W. Bromiley. Edited by G. W. Bromiley and T. F. Torrance. Edinburgh: T&T Clark, 1956.

Barth, Karl. *Church Dogmatics, IV/2*. Translated by G. W. Bromiley. Edited by G. W. Bromiley and T. F. Torrance. Edinburgh: T&T Clark, 1958.

Barth, Karl. *Church Dogmatics, IV/3.1*. Translated by G. W. Bromiley. Edited by G. W. Bromiley and T. F. Torrance. Edinburgh: T&T Clark, 1961.

Barth, Karl. *Church Dogmatics, IV/3.2*. Translated by G. W. Bromiley. Edited by G. W. Bromiley and T. F. Torrance. Edinburgh: T&T Clark, 1962.

Beilby, James K. and Paul R. Eddy, Eds. *Divine Foreknowledge: Four Views*. Downers Grove, IL: InterVarsity Press, 2001.

Bonner, Gerald. *Freedom and Necessity: St. Augustine's Teaching on Divine Power and Human Freedom*. Washington, DC: Catholic University of America Press, 2007.

Butterfield, Herbert. *Christianity and History*. London: Fontana Books, 1958.

Calvin, John. *The Bondage and Liberation of the Will: A Defence of the Orthodox Doctrine of Human Choice against Pighius*. Translated by Graham I. Davies. Edited by A. N. S. Lane. Grand Rapids, MI: Baker Books, 1996.

Calvin, John. *Concerning the Eternal Predestination of God*. Translated by J. K. S. Reid. Louisville, KY: Westminster John Knox Press, 1997.

Calvin, John. *Institutes of the Christian Religion*. Translated by Ford Lewis Battles. The Library of Christian Classics, Vol. 20. Edited by John T. McNeill. Philadelphia, PA: Westminster Press, 1960.

Chiang, Ted. "Hell Is the Absence of God." In *Stories of Your Life and Others*. New York: Vintage Books, 2002, pp. 205–35.

Cillis, Maria De. *Free Will and Predestination in Islamic Thought: Theoretical Compromises in the Works of Avicenna, al-Ghazali and Ibn 'Arabi*. New York: Routledge, 2013.

Clarke, Arthur C. *Childhood's End*. New York: Ballantine Books, 1953.

Couenhoven, Jesse. "Augustine's Rejection of the Free Will Defence: An Overview of the Late Augustine's Theodicy." *Religious Studies* 43 (2007): 279–98.

Couenhoven, Jesse. "Augustine of Hippo." In *The Routledge Companion to Free Will*. Edited by Kevin Timpe, Meghan Griffith, and Neil Levy. New York: Routledge, 2016, pp. 247–57.

Couenhoven, Jesse. "Augustine, Saint." In *International Encyclopedia of Ethics*. Edited by Hugh LaFollette. Malden, MA: Blackwell Press, 2013, pp. 399–407.

Couenhoven, Jesse. "Karl Barth's Conception(s) of Human and Divine Freedom(s)." In *Commanding Grace: Studies in Barth's Ethics*. Edited by Daniel Migliore. Grand Rapids, MI: William B. Eerdmans, 2010, pp. 239–55.

Couenhoven, Jesse. "The Necessities of Perfect Freedom." *International Journal of Systematic Theology* 14, no. 4 (2012): 396–419.

Couenhoven, Jesse. *Stricken by Sin, Cured by Christ: Agency, Necessity, and Culpability in Augustinian Theology*. New York: Oxford Unversity Press, 2013.

Dunne, John, ed. *Poems of John Donne. vol I.* Edited by E. K. Chambers. London: Lawrence & Bullen, 1896.

Fischer, John Martin, Robert Kane, Derk Pereboom, and Manuel Vargas. *Four Views on Free Will.* Malden, MA: Blackwell, 2007.

Godsey, John, ed. *Karl Barth's Table Talk.* Richmond, VA: John Knox Press, 1963.

Haji, Ishtiyaque. *Moral Appraisability: Puzzles, Proposals, and Perplexities.* New York: Oxford University Press, 1998.

Hasker, William. *Providence, Evil, and the Openness of God.* New York: Routledge, 2004.

Hector, Kevin W. "God's Triunity and Self-Determination: A Conversation with Karl Barth, Bruce McCormack and Paul Molnar." *International Journal of Systematic Theology* 7, no. 3 (2005): 246–61.

Helm, Paul. "Calvin the Compatibilist." In *Calvin at the Centre.* New York: Oxford University Press, 2010, pp. 227–72.

Helm, Paul. *John Calvin's Ideas.* New York: Oxford University Press, 2004.

Hoffman, Tobias, and Peter Furlong. "Free Choice." In *Aquinas's Disputed Questions on Evil: A Critical Guide.* Edited by M. V. Dougherty. New York: Cambridge University Press, 2015, pp. 56–74.

Hunsinger, George. *Reading Barth with Charity: A Hermeneutical Proposal.* Grand Rapids, MI: Baker Academic, 2015.

Klawans, Jonathan. *Josephus and the Theologies of Ancient Judaism.* New York: Oxford University Press, 2012.

Kolb, Robert. *Bound Choice, Election, and Wittenberg Theological Method: From Martin Luther to the Formula of Concord.* Grand Rapids, MI: William B. Eerdmans Publishing Company, 2005.

Langer, Ellen J. "The Illusion of Control." *Journal of Personality and Social Psychology* 32, no. 2 (1975): 311–28.

Levering, Matthew. *Predestination: Biblical and Theological Paths.* New York: Oxford University Press, 2011.

Lewis, C. S. "The Four Loves." In *The Inspirational Writings of C. S. Lewis.* New York: Inspirational Press, 2004.

Lewis, C. S. *The Great Divorce.* New York: HarperOne, 2009.

Luther, Martin. *The Bondage of the Will.* Translated by Philip S. Watson and Benjamin Drewery. *Luther's Works, Career of the Reformer III: Vol 33.* Edited by Helmut T. Lehmann. Philadelphia, PA: Fortress Press, 1972.

Luther, Martin. "Disputation Against Scholastic Theology." Translated by Harold J. Grimm. In *Luther's Works, Volume 31: Career of the Reformer I.* Edited by Helmut T. Lehmann and Harold J. Grimm. Philadelphia, PA: Fortress Press, 1957, pp. 3–16.

Luther, Martin. *The Freedom of a Christian.* Translated by W. A. Lambert and Revised by Harold J. Grimm. *Martin Luther, Selections from His*

Writings. Edited by John Dillenberger. Philadelphia, PA: Fortress Press, 1951, pp. 42–85.

Luther, Martin. "Heidelberg Disputation." Translated by Harold J. Grimm. Chap. 35–70. In *Luther's Works, Volume 31: Career of the Reformer I*. Edited by Helmut T. Lehmann and Harold J. Grimm. Philadelphia, PA: Fortress Press, 1957, pp. 35–70.

Luther, Martin. *Lectures on Galations 1535: Chapters 1–4. Luther's Works, Vol 26*. Edited and Translated by Jaroslav Pelican. Saint Louis, MI: Concordia Publishing House, 1963.

Luther, Martin. *Lectures on Genesis*. Translated by George V. Schick and Paul D. Pahl. *Luther's Works Vol. 5*. Edited by Jaroslav Pelican. Saint Louis, MO: Concordia Publishing House, 1968.

Luther, Martin. *Lectures on Romans*. Translated by Walter G. Tillmanns and Jacob A. O. Preus. *Luther's Works Vol. 25*. Edited by Jaroslav Pelican. Saint Louis, MO: Concordia Publishing House, 1972.

Luther, Martin. "Letter to Wolfgang Capito, July 9, 1537." Translated by Gottfried G. Krodel. In *Luther's Works, Vol 50. Letters III*. Edited by Helmut T. Lehmann. Philadelphia, PA: Fortress Press, 1974, pp. 171–3.

Małysz, Piotr J. "Martin Luther's Trinitarian Hermeneutic of Freedom." In *Oxford Research Encyclopedia of Religion*. Edited by John Barton. New York: Oxford University Press, 2017.

Meilaender, Gilbert. "The Examined Life Is Not Worth Living: Learning from Luther." In *The Theory and Practice Of Virtue*. South Bend, IN: University of Notre Dame Press, 1988, pp. 100–26.

Miller, Christian B. *Character and Moral Psychology*. New York: Oxford University Press, 2014.

Milton, John. *Paradise Lost*. Edited by Barbara K. Lewalski. New York: Blackwell, 2007.

Murdoch, Iris. *The Sovereignty of Good*. New York: Routledge, 1970.

Nagel, Thomas. "Moral Luck." In *Mortal Questions*. New York: Cambridge University Press, 1979, pp. 24–38.

Pasnau, Robert. "Snatching Hope from the Jaws of Epistemic Defeat." *Journal of the American Philosophical Association* 1, no. 2 (2015): 257–75.

Pasnau, Robert. *Thomas Aquinas on Human Nature*. New York: Cambridge University Press, 2002.

Pereboom, Derk. "Theological Determinism and the Relationship with God." In *Free Will and Classical Theism: The Significance of Freedom in Perfect Being Theology*. Edited by Hugh J. McCann. New York: Oxford University Press, 2017, pp. 201–19.

Rogers, Katherin. *Anselm on Freedom*. New York: Oxford University Press, 2008.

Russell, Paul. "Compatibilist-Fatalism." In *Moral Responsibility and Ontology*. Edited by Ton van den Beld. Boston, MA: Kluwer Academic Publishers, 2000, pp. 199–218.

Sanders, John. *The God Who Risks: A Theology of Providence*. Downers Grove, IL: InterVarsity Press, 1998.

Scanlon, T. M. "Reasons and Passions." In *The Contours of Agency*. Edited by Sarah Buss and Lee Overton. Cambridge, MA: The MIT Press, 2002, pp. 165–83.

Schleiermacher, Friedrich. *On the Doctrine of Election, with Special Reference to the Aphorisms of Dr. Bretschneider*. Translated by Iain G. Nicol and Allen G. Jorgenson. Louisville, KY: Westminster John Knox Press, 2012.

Schlossberger, Eugene. *Moral Responsibility and Persons*. Philadelphia, PA: Temple University Press, 1992.

Stump, Eleonore. *Aquinas*. New York: Routledge, 2005.

Tanner, Kathryn. *God and Creation in Christian Theology: Tyranny or Empowerment?* Minneapolis, MN: Fortress Press, 2004.

Thompson, Suzanne C. "Illusions of Control: How We Overestimate Our Personal Influence." *Current Directions in Psychological Science* 8 (1999): 187–90.

Thuesen, Peter J. *Predestination: The American Career of a Contentious Doctrine*. New York: Oxford University Press, 2009.

Timpe, Kevin. *Free Will: Sourcehood and Its Alternatives*. New York: Continuum, 2008.

van Inwagen, Peter. "When the Will is Not Free." *Philosophical Studies* 75 (1994): 95–113.

Visser, Sandra. "Anselm of Canterbury." In *The Routledge Companion to Free Will*. Edited by Neil Levy, Meghan Griffith, and Kevin Timpe. New York: Routledge, 2016, pp. 258–64.

Watson, Gary. "Responsibility and the Limits of Evil: Variations on a Strawsonian Theme." In *Responsibility, Character, and the Emotions*. Edited by Ferdinand Schoeman. New York: Cambridge University Press, 1987, pp. 256–86.

INDEX